CLOUD

9

N
H
B

NICK HERN BOOKS

A Nick Hern Book

This edition of *Cloud Nine* first published in 1989
by Nick Hern Books

Reprinted 1994, 1997, 1998, 2000, 2001, 2002, 2003, 2004 (twice) by
Nick Hern Books Limited,
14 Larden Road, London W3 7ST

Cloud Nine first published in Great Britain in 1979 by
Pluto Press Ltd. and Joint Stock Theatre Group; Second Ed.
1980, Third Ed. 1983; Fourth Ed. (revised) 1984. Published
in Methuen's World Dramatists anthology edition 1985

Copyright © 1979, 1980, 1983, 1984, 1985 by Caryl Churchill

Lyrics: *Come Gather Sons of England* copyright © 1902
by Anthony Wilkin; *A Boy's Best Friend* copyright © 1897
by Joseph D. Skelly; *Cloud Nine* © 1979 by Caryl Churchill
and Andy Roberts

Front cover illustration: details from
Top: Uniform section of *Encyclopaedia Britannica* 1911 Ed.
Middle: *Venus* 1918 by Modigliani from the Galerie Alex Magny,
    Paris
Bottom: Self Portrait with Badges, 1961, by Peter Blake
Reproduced by courtesy of the Trustees of the Tate Gallery

Set in Baskerville by Book Ens, Saffron Walden, Essex.
Printed by Cox & Wyman Ltd, Reading, Berkshire.

British Library Cataloguing in Publication Data
Churchill, Caryl
   Cloud nine
   I. Title
   822'.914
   ISBN 1-85459-090-1

Caryl Churchill: a Chronology of Performed Plays

Play	Written	Performed
		(s: *stage*, r: *radio*, t: *television*)
Downstairs	1958	1958s
You've No Need to be Frightened	1959?	1961r
Having a Wonderful Time	1959	1960s
Easy Death	1960	1961s
The Ants	1961	1962r
Lovesick	1965	1966r
Identical Twins	?	1968r
Abortive	1968?	1971r
Not . . . not . . . not . . . not . . . not Enough Oxygen	?	1971r
Schreber's Nervous Illness	?	1972r
Henry's Past	1971	1972r
The Judge's Wife	1971?	1972t
Owners	1972	1972s
Moving Clocks Go Slow	1973	1975s
Turkish Delight	1973	1974t
Perfect Happiness	1973	1973r
Objections to Sex and Violence	1974	1975s
Traps	1976	1977s
Vinegar Tom	1976	1976s
Light Shining in Buckinghamshire	1976	1976s
Floorshow (contributor to)	1977	1977s
The After Dinner Joke	1977	1978t
The Legion Hall Bombing	1978	1979t
Softcops	1978	1983s
Cloud Nine	1978	1979s
Three More Sleepless Nights	1979	1980s
Crimes	1981	1981t
Top Girls	1980-2	1982s
Fen	1982	1983s
A Mouthful of Birds (with David Lan)	1986	1986s
Serious Money	1987	1987s
Icecream	1988	1989s
Mad Forest	1989	1990s
Lives of the Great Poisoners	1990	1991s
The Skriker	1992	1994s
Thyestes (translated from Seneca)	1992	1994s
Hotel	1995	1997s
Blue Heart	1996	1997s
Far Away	2000	2000s
A Number	2002	2002s

Cloud Nine

Cloud Nine was written for Joint Stock Theatre Group in 1978-79. The company's usual work method is to set up a workshop in which the writer, director and actors research a particular subject. The writer then goes away to write the play, before returning to the company for a rehearsal and rewrite period. In the case of *Cloud Nine* the workshop lasted for three weeks, the writing period for twelve, and the rehearsal for six.

The workshop for *Cloud Nine* was about sexual politics. This meant that the starting point for our research was to talk about ourselves and share our very different attitudes and experiences. We also explored stereotypes and role reversals in games and improvisations, read books and talked to other people. Though the play's situations and characters were not developed in the workshop, it draws deeply on this material, and I wouldn't have written the same play without it.

When I came to write the play, I returned to an idea that had been touched on briefly in the workshop – the parallel between colonial and sexual oppression, which Genet calls 'the colonial or feminine mentality of interiorised repression'. So the first act of *Cloud Nine* takes place in Victorian Africa, where Clive, the white man, imposes his ideals on his family and the natives. Betty, Clive's wife, is played by a man because she wants to be what men want her to be, and, in the same way, Joshua, the black servant, is played by a white man because he wants to be what whites want him to be. Betty does not value herself as a woman, nor does Joshua value himself as a black. Edward, Clive's son, is played by a woman for a different reason – partly to do with the stage convention of having boys played by women (Peter Pan, radio plays, etc.) and partly with highlighting the way Clive tries to impose traditional male behaviour on him. Clive struggles throughout the act to maintain the world he wants to see – a faithful wife, a manly

LIN. You said call up the goddess.

EDWARD. I don't remember saying that.

LIN. We could have called her on the telephone.

EDWARD. Don't be so silly, this is meant to be frightening.

LIN. Kiss me.

VICTORIA. Are we going to do it?

LIN. We're doing it.

VICTORIA. A ceremony.

LIN. It's very sexy, you said it is. You said the women were priests in the temples and fucked all the time. I'm just helping.

VICTORIA. As long as it's sacred.

LIN. It's very sacred.

VICTORIA. Innin, Innana, Nana, Nut, Anat, Anahita, Istar, Isis.

LIN. I can't remember all that.

VICTORIA. Lin! Innin, Innana, Nana, Nut, Anat, Anahita, Istar, Isis.

> LIN *and* EDWARD *join in and continue the chant under* VICTORIA's *speech.*
> Goddess of many names, oldest of the old, who walked in chaos and created life, hear us calling you back through time, before Jehovah, before Christ, before men drove you out and burnt your temples, hear us, Lady, give us back what we were, give us the history we haven't had, make us the women we can't be.

> ALL: Innin, Innana, Nana, Nut, Anat, Anahita, Istar, Isis.

> *Chant continues under other speeches.*

LIN. Come back, goddess.

VICTORIA. Goddess of the sun and the moon her brother,

little goddess of Crete with snakes in your hands.

LIN.   Goddess of breasts.

VICTORIA.   Goddess of cunts.

LIN.   Goddess of fat bellies and babies. And blood blood blood.

Chant continues.

I see her.

EDWARD.   What?

They stop chanting.

LIN.   I see her. Very tall. Snakes in her hands. Light light light – look out! Did I give you a fright?

EDWARD.   I was terrified.

VICTORIA.   Don't spoil it Lin.

LIN.   It's all out of a book.

VICTORIA.   Innin Innana – I can't do it now. I was really enjoying myself.

LIN.   She won't appear with a man here.

VICTORIA.   They had men, they had sons and lovers.

EDWARD.   They had eunuchs.

LIN.   Don't give us ideas.

VICTORIA.   There's Attis and Tammuz, they're torn to pieces.

EDWARD.   Tear me to pieces, Lin.

VICTORIA.   The priestess chose a lover for a year and he was king because she chose him and then he was killed at the end of the year.

EDWARD.   Hurray.

VICTORIA.   And the women had the children and nobody knew it was done by fucking so they didn't know about their fathers and nobody cared who the father was and the property was passed down through the maternal line—

LIN.   Don't turn it into a lecture, Vicky, it's meant
              to be an orgy.

VICTORIA.   It never hurts to understand the theoretical
              background. You can't separate fucking and
              economics.

LIN.   Give us a kiss.

EDWARD.   Shut up, listen.

LIN.   What?

EDWARD.   There's somebody there.

LIN.   Where?

EDWARD.   There.

VICTORIA.   The priestesses used to make love to total
              strangers.

LIN.   Go on then, I dare you.

EDWARD.   Go on, Vicky.

VICTORIA.   He won't know it's a sacred rite in honour of
              the goddess.

EDWARD.   We'll know.

LIN.   We can tell him.

EDWARD.   It's not what he thinks, it's what we think.

LIN.   Don't tell him till after, he'll run a mile.

VICTORIA.   Hello. We're having an orgy. Do you want me
              to suck your cock?

              The stranger approaches. It is MARTIN.

MARTIN.   There you are. I've been looking everywhere.
              What the hell are you doing. Do you know
              what the time is? You're all pissed out of your
              minds.

              They leap on MARTIN, *and pull him down and
              start to make love to him.*

MARTIN.   Well that's all right. If all we're talking about is
              having a lot of sex there's no problem. I was
              all for the sixties when liberation just meant
              fucking.

Another stranger approaches.

LIN.   Hey you, come here. Come and have sex with
            us.

VICTORIA.   Who is it?

            The stranger is a soldier.

LIN.   It's my brother.

EDWARD.   Lin, don't.

LIN.   It's my brother.

VICTORIA.   It's her sense of humour, you get used to it.

LIN.   Shut up Vicky, it's my brother. Isn't it? Bill?

SOLDIER.   Yes it's me.

LIN.   And you are dead.

SOLDIER.   Fucking dead all right yeh.

LIN.   Have you come back to tell us something?

SOLDIER.   No I've come for a fuck. That was the worst
            thing in the fucking army. Never fucking let
            out. Can't fucking talk to Irish girls. Fucking
            bored out of my fucking head. That or shit
            scared. For five minutes I'd be glad I wasn't
            bored, then I was fucking scaed. Then we'd
            come in and I'd be glad I wasn't scared and
            then I was fucking bored. Spend the day
            reading fucking porn and the fucking night
            wanking. Man's fucking life in the fucking
            army? No fun when the fucking kids hate you.
            I got so I fucking wanted to kill someone and
            I got fucking killed myself and I want a fuck.

LIN.   I miss you. Bill. Bill.

            LIN *collapses.* SOLDIER *goes.* VICTORIA
            comforts LIN.

EDWARD.   Let's go home.

LIN.   Victoria, come home with us. Victoria's
            coming to live with me and Edward.

MARTIN.   Tell me about it in the morning.

LIN.   It's true.

VICTORIA. It is true.

MARTIN.   Tell me when you're sober.

EDWARD, LIN, VICTORIA *go off together.*
MARTIN *goes off alone.* GERRY *comes on.*

GERRY.   I come here sometimes at night and pick
            somebody up. Sometimes I come here at night
            and don't pick anybody up. I do also enjoy
            walking about at night. There's never any
            trouble finding someone. I can have sex any
            time. You might not find the type you most
            fancy every day of the week, but there's plenty
            of people about who just enjoy having a good
            time. I quite like living alone. If I live with
            someone I get annoyed with them. Edward
            always put on Capital radio when he got up.
            The silence gets wasted. I wake up at four
            o'clock sometimes. Birds. Silence. If I bring
            somebody home I never let them stay the
            night. Edward! Edward!

            EDWARD *from Act One comes on.*

EDWARD.   Gerry, I love you.

GERRY.   Yes, I know. I love you, too.

EDWARD.   You know what we did? I want to do it again.
            I think about it all the time. Don't you want to
            any more?

GERRY.   Yes, of course.

ALL (*sing 'Cloud Nine'*).

It'll be find when you reach Cloud Nine.

Mist was rising and the night was dark.
Me and my baby took a walk in the park.
He said Be mine and you're on Cloud Nine.

Better watch out when you're on Cloud Nine.

Smoked some dope on the playground swings
Higher and higher on true love's wings
He said be mine and you're on Cloud Nine.

Twenty-five years on the same Cloud Nine.

Who did she meet on her first blind date?
The guys were no surprise but the lady was great
They were women in love, they were on Cloud Nine.

Two the same, they were on Cloud Nine.

The bride was sixty-five, the groom was seventeen,
They fucked in the back of the black limousine.
It was divine in the silver Cloud Nine.

Simply divine in their silver Cloud Nine.

The wife's lover's children and my lover's wife,
Cooking in my kitchen, confusing my life.
And it's upside down when you reach Cloud Nine.

Upside down when you reach Cloud Nine.

Scene Four

The park. Afternoon in late summer. MARTIN, CATHY,
EDWARD.

CATHY.   Under the bramble bushes,
           Under the sea boom boom boom,
           True love for you my darling,
           True love for me my darling,
           When we are married,
           We'll raise a family.
           Boy for you, girl for me,
           Boom Tiddley oom boom.
           SEXY.

EDWARD.   You'll have Tommy and Cathy tonight then
           OK? Tommy's still on antibiotics, do make
           him finish the bottle, he takes it in Ribena. It's
           no good in orange, he spits it out. Remind me
           to give you Cathy's swimming things.

CATHY.   I did six strokes, didn't I Martin? Did I do a
           width? How many strokes is a length? How
           many miles is a swimming pool? I'm going to
           take my bronze and silver and gold and
           diamond.

MARTIN. Is Tommy still wetting the bed?

EDWARD. Don't get angry with him about it.

MARTIN. I just need to go to the launderette so I've got a spare sheet. Of course I don't get fucking angry, Eddy, for God's sake. I don't like to say he is my son but he is my son. I'm surprised I'm not wetting the bed myself.

CATHY. I don't wet the bed ever. Do you wet the bed Martin?

MARTIN. No.

CATHY. You said you did.

BETTY *comes.*

BETTY. I do miss the sun living in England but today couldn't be more beautiful. You appreciate the weekend when you're working. Betty's been at work this week, Cathy. It's terribly tiring, Martin, I don't know how you've done it all these years. And the money, I feel like a child with money, Clive always paid everything but I do understand it perfectly well. Look, Cathy, let me show you my money.

CATHY. I'll count it. Let me count it. What's that?

BETTY. Five pounds. Five and five is—?

CATHY. One two three—

BETTY. Five and five is ten, and five—

CATHY. If I get it right can I have one?

EDWARD. No you can't.

CATHY *goes on counting the money.*

BETTY. I never like to say anything, Martin, or you'll think I'm being a mother-in-law.

EDWARD. Which you are.

BETTY. Thank you, Edward, I'm not talking to you. Martin, I think you're being wonderful. Vicky will come back. Just let her stay with Lin till she sorts herself out. It's very nice for a girl to have a friend, I had friends at school, that was very nice. But I'm sure Lin and Edward don't want her with them all the time. I'm not at all shocked that Lin and Edward aren't married and she already has a child, we all know first marriages don't always work out. But really Vicky must be in the way. And poor little Tommy. I hear he doesn't sleep properly and he's had a cough.

MARTIN.   No, he's fine, Betty, thank you.

CATHY.   My bed's horrible. I want to sleep in the big bed with Lin and Vicky and Eddy and I do get in if I've got a bad dream, and my bed's got a bump right in my back. I want to sleep in a tent.

BETTY.   Well Tommy has got a nasty cough, Martin, whatever you say.

EDWARD.   He's over that. He's got some medicine.

MARTIN.   He takes it in Ribena.

BETTY.   Well I'm glad to hear it. Look what a lot of money, Cathy, and I sit behind a desk on my own and I answer the telephone and keep the doctor's appointment book and it really is great fun.

CATHY.   Can we go camping, Martin, in a tent? We could take the Dead Hand Gang.

BETTY.   Not those big boys, Cathy? They're far too big and rough for you. They climb back into the park after dark. I'm sure mummy doesn't let you play with them, does she Edward? Well I don't know.

Ice cream bells.

CATHY.   Ice cream. Martin you promised. I'll have a double ninety-nine. No I'll have a shandy lolly. Betty, you have a shandy lolly and I'll have a lick. No, you have a double ninety-nine and I'll have the chocolate.

MARTIN, CATHY *and* BETTY *go, leaving*
EDWARD. GERRY *comes.*

GERRY. Hello, Eddy. Thought I might find you here.

EDWARD. Gerry.

GERRY. Not working today then?

EDWARD. I don't work here any more.

GERRY. Your mum got you into a dark suit?

EDWARD. No of course not. I'm on the dole. I am
working, though, I do housework.

GERRY. Whose wife are you now then?

EDWARD. Nobody's. I don't think like that any more.
I'm living with some women.

GERRY. What women?

EDWARD. It's my sister, Vic, and her lover. They go out
to work and I look after the kids.

GERRY. I thought for a moment you said you were
living with women.

EDWARD. We do sleep together, yes.

GERRY. I was passing the park anyway so I thought I'd
look in. I was in the sauna the other night and
I saw someone who looked like you but it
wasn't. I had sex with him anyway.

EDWARD. I do go to the sauna sometimes.

CATHY *comes, gives* EDWARD *an ice cream, goes.*

GERRY. I don't think I'd like living with children. They
make a lot of noise don't they?

EDWARD. I tell them to shut up and they shut up. I
wouldn't want to leave them at the moment.

GERRY. Look why don't we go for a meal sometime?

EDWARD. Yes I'd like that. Where are you living now?

GERRY. Same place.

EDWARD. I'll come round for you tomorrow night about
7.30.

GERRY.   Great.

            EDWARD *goes.* HARRY *comes.* HARRY *and*
            GERRY *pick each other up. They go off.* BETTY
            comes back.

BETTY.   No, the ice cream was my treat, Martin. Off
            you go. I'm going to have a quiet sit in the
            sun.

            MAUD *comes.*

MAUD.   Let Mrs Saunders be a warning to you, Betty. I
            know what it is to be unprotected.

BETTY.   But mother, I have a job. I earn money.

MAUD.   I know we have our little differences but I
            always want what is best for you.

            ELLEN *comes.*

ELLEN.   Betty, what happens with a man?

BETTY.   You just keep still.

ELLEN.   And is it enjoyable? Don't forget me, Betty.

            MAUD *and* ELLEN *go.*

BETTY.   I used to think Clive was the one who liked
            sex. But then I found I missed it. I used to
            touch myself when I was very little, I thought
            I'd invented something wonderful. I used to
            do it to go to sleep with or to cheer myself up,
            and one day it was raining and I was under
            the kitchen table, and my mother saw me with
            my hand under my dress rubbing away, and
            she dragged me out so quickly I hit my head
            and it bled and I was sick, and nothing was
            said, and I never did it again till this year. I
            thought if Clive wasn't looking at me there
            wasn't a person there. And one night in bed in
            my flat I was so frightened I started touching
            myself. I thought my hand might go through
            space. I touched my face, it was there, my
            arm, my breast, and my hand went down
            where I thought it shouldn't, and I thought
            well there is somebody there. It felt very sweet,

it was a feeling from very long ago, it was very
soft, just barely touching, and I felt myself
gathering together more and more and I felt
angry with Clive and angry with my mother
and I went on and on defying them, and there
was this vast feeling growing in me and all
round me and they couldn't stop me and no
one could stop me and I was there and
coming and coming. Afterwards I thought I'd
betrayed Clive. My mother would kill me. But
I felt triumphant because I was a separate
person from them. And I cried because I
didn't want to be. But I don't cry about it any
more. Sometimes I do it three times in one
night and it really is great fun.

VICTORIA *and* LIN *come in.*

VICTORIA. So I said to the professor, I don't think this is
an occasion for invoking the concept of
structural causality—oh hello mummy.

BETTY. I'm going to ask you a question, both of you.
I have a little money from your grandmother.
And the three of you are living in that tiny flat
with two children. I wonder if we could get a
house and all live in it together? It would give
you more room.

VICTORIA. But I'm going to Manchester anyway.

LIN. We'd have a garden, Vicky.

BETTY. You do seem to have such fun all of you.

VICTORIA. I don't want to.

BETTY. I didn't think you would.

LIN. Come on, Vicky, she knows we sleep together,
and Eddy.

BETTY. I think I've known for quite a while but I'm
not sure. I don't usually think about it, so I
don't know if I know about it or not.

VICTORIA. I don't want to live with my mother.

LIN. Don't think of her as your mother, think of
her as Betty.

VICTORIA. But she thinks of herself as my mother.

BETTY. I am your mother.

VICTORIA. But mummy we don't even like each other.

BETTY. We might begin to.

CATHY *comes on howling with a nosebleed.*

LIN. Oh Cathy what happened?

BETTY. She's been assaulted.

VICTORIA. It's a nosebleed.

CATHY. Took my ice cream.

LIN. Who did?

CATHY. Took my money.

MARTIN *comes.*

MARTIN. Is everything all right?

LIN. I thought you were looking after her.

CATHY. They hit me. I can't play. They said I'm a girl.

BETTY. Those dreadful boys, the gang, the Dead Hand.

MARTIN. What do you mean you thought I was looking after her?

LIN. Last I saw her she was with you getting an ice cream. It's your afternoon.

MARTIN. Then she went off to play. She goes off to play. You don't keep an eye on her every minute.

LIN. She doesn't get beaten up when I'm looking after her.

CATHY. Took my money.

MARTIN. Why the hell should I look after your child anyway? I just want Tommy. Why should he live with you and Vicky all week?

LIN. I don't mind if you don't want to look after her but don't say you will and then this happens.

VICTORIA. When I get to Manchester everything's going to be different anyway, Lin's staying here, and

you're staying here, we're all going to have to
sit down and talk it through.

MARTIN.   I'd really enjoy that.

CATHY.   Hit me on the face.

LIN.   You were the one looking after her and look at
her now, that's all.

MARTIN.   I've had enough of you telling me.

LIN.   Yes you know it all.

MARTIN.   Now stop it. I work very hard at not being like
this, I could do with some credit.

LIN.   OK you're quite nice, try and enjoy it. Don't
make me sorry for you, Martin, it's hard for me
too. We've better things to do than quarrel. I've
got to go and sort those little bastards out for a
start. Where are they, Cathy?

CATHY.   Don't kill them, mum, hit them. Give them a
nosebleed, mum.

           LIN *goes*.

VICTORIA. Tommy's asleep in the pushchair. We'd better
wake him up or he won't sleep tonight.

MARTIN.   Sometimes I keep him up watching television till
he falls asleep on the sofa so I can hold him.
Come on, Cathy, we'll get another ice cream.

CATHY.   Chocolate sauce and nuts.

VICTORIA. Betty, would you like an ice cream?

BETTY.   No thank you, the cold hurts my teeth, but what
a nice thought, Vicky, thank you.

           VICTORIA *goes*. BETTY *alone*. GERRY *comes*.

BETTY.   I think you used to be Edward's flatmate.

GERRY.   You're his mother. He's talked about you.

BETTY.   Well never mind. Children are always wrong
about their parents. It's a great problem
knowing where to live and who to share with. I
live by myself just now.

GERRY.   Good, so do I. You can do what you like.

BETTY.   I don't really know what I like.

GERRY.   You'll soon find out.

BETTY.   What do you like?

GERRY.   Waking up at four in the morning.

BETTY.   I like listening to music in bed and sometimes
          for supper I just have a big piece of bread and
          dip it in very hot lime pickle. So you don't get
          lonely by yourself? Perhaps you have a lot of
          visitors. I've been thinking I should have some
          visitors, I could give a little dinner party.
          Would you come? There wouldn't just be
          bread and lime pickle.

GERRY.   Thank you very much.

BETTY.   Or don't wait to be asked to dinner. Just drop
          in informally. I'll give you the address shall I?
          I don't usually give strange men my address
          but then you're not a strange man, you're a
          friend of Edward's. I suppose I seem a
          different generation to you but you are older
          than Edward. I was married for so many years
          it's quite hard to know how to get acquainted.
          But if there isn't a right way to do things you
          have to invent one. I always thought my
          mother was far too old to be attractive but
          when you get to an age yourself it feels quite
          different.

GERRY.   I think you could be quite attractive.

BETTY.   If what?

GERRY.   If you stop worrying.

BETTY.   I think when I do more about things I worry
          about them less. So perhaps you could help me
          do more.

GERRY.   I might be going to live with Edward again.

BETTY.   That's nice, but I'm rather surprised if he wants
          to share a flat. He's rather involved with a
          young woman he lives with, or two young

son. Harry's homosexuality is reviled, Ellen's is invisible. Rehearsing the play for the first time, we were initially taken by how funny the first act was and then by the painfulness of the relationships – which then became more funny than when they had seemed purely farcical.

The second act is set in London in 1979 – this is where I wanted the play to end up, in the changing sexuality of our own time. Betty is middle-aged, Edward and Victoria have grown up. A hundred years have passed, but for the characters only twenty-five years. There were two reasons for this. I felt the first act would be stronger set in Victorian times, at the height of colonialism, rather than in Africa during the 1950s. And when the company talked about their childhoods and the attitudes to sex and marriage that they had been given when they were young, everyone felt that they had received very conventional, almost Victorian expectations and that they had made great changes and discoveries in their lifetimes.

The first act, like the society it shows, is male dominated and firmly structured. In the second act, more energy comes from the women and the gays. The uncertainties and changes of society, and a more feminine and less authoritarian feeling, are reflected in the looser structure of the act. Betty, Edward and Victoria all change from the rigid positions they had been left in by the first act, partly because of their encounters with Gerry and Lin.

In fact, all the characters in this act change a little for the better. If men are finding it hard to keep control in the first act, they are finding it hard to let go in the second: Martin dominates Victoria, despite his declarations of sympathy for feminism, and the bitter end of colonialism is apparent in Lin's soldier brother, who dies in Northern Ireland. Betty is now played by a woman, as she gradually becomes real to herself. Cathy is played by a man, partly as a simple reversal of Edward being played by a woman, partly because the size and presence of a man on stage seemed appropriate to the emotional force of young children, and partly, as with Edward, to show more clearly the issues involved in learning what is considered correct behaviour for a girl.

It is essential for Joshua to be played by a white, Betty (I) by a man, Edward (I) by a woman, and Cathy by a man.

The soldier should be played by the actor who plays Cathy. The doubling of Mrs Saunders and Ellen is not intended to make a point so much as for sheer fun – and of course to keep the company to seven in each act. The doubling can be done in any way that seems right for any particular production. The first production went Clive-Cathy, Betty-Edward, Edward-Betty, Maud-Victoria, Mrs Saunders/Ellen-Lin, Joshua-Gerry, Harry-Martin. When we did the play again, at the Royal Court in 1980, we decided to try a different doubling: Clive-Edward, Betty-Gerry, Edward-Victoria, Maud-Lin, Mrs Saunders/Ellen-Betty, Joshua-Cathy, Harry-Martin. I've a slight preference for the first way because I like seeing Clive become Cathy, and enjoy the Edward-Betty connections. Some doublings aren't practicable, but any way of doing the doubling seems to set up some interesting resonances between the two acts. Gerry's age, referred to as 32 in the text, can be altered to fit the actor.

C.C. 1983

The Text

The first edition of *Cloud Nine* (Pluto/Joint Stock 1979) went to
press before the end of rehearsal. Further changes were made
within the first week or two of production, and these were
incorporated in the Pluto/Joint Stock/Royal Court edition
1980. This edition also went to press during rehearsal, so
although it may include some small changes made for that
production, others don't turn up till the Pluto Plays edition
1983, which also includes a few changes from the American
production, a few lines cut here or reinstated there. Other
changes for the American production can be found in French's
American acting edition – the main ones are the position of
Betty's monologue and some lines of the 'ghosts'. For the
Fireside Bookclub and Methuen Inc (1984) in America I did
another brushing up, not very different from Pluto '83, and
I have kept almost the same text for this edition.

There's a problem with the Maud and Ellen reappearances in
Act Two. If Ellen is doubled with Betty, obviously only Maud
can appear. Equally Maud-Betty would mean only Ellen could,
though that seems a dull doubling. This text gives both Maud
and Ellen. In the production at the Court in 1981 only Maud
appeared and she has some extra lines so she can talk about sex
as well as work; they can be found in Pluto 1983.

C.C. 1984

Cloud Nine was first performed at Dartington College of Arts on Wednesday 14 February 1979 by the Joint Stock Theatre Group, then on tour and at the Royal Court Theatre, London, with the following cast:

Act One

CLIVE, a colonial administrator	Antony Sher
BETTY, his wife, played by a man	Jim Hooper
JOSHUA, his black servant, played by a white	Tony Rohr
EDWARD, his son, played by a woman	Julie Covington
MAUD, his mother-in-law	Miriam Margolyes
ELLEN, Edward's governess / MRS SAUNDERS, a widow	Carole Hayman
HARRY BAGLEY, an explorer	William Hoyland

Act Two

BETTY	Julie Covington
EDWARD, her son	Jim Hooper
VICTORIA, her daughter	Miriam Margolyes
MARTIN, Victoria's husband	William Hoyland
LIN	Carole Hayman
CATHY, Lin's daughter aged 4 and 5, played by a man	Antony Sher
GERRY, Edward's lover	Tony Rohr

Director: Max Stafford-Clark
Assistant Director: Les Waters
Designer: Peter Hartwell
Musical Director: Andy Roberts
Lighting Director: Robin Myerscough-Walker

Except for Cathy, characters in Act II are played by actors of their own sex.

Act One takes place in a British colony in Africa in Victorian times. Act Two takes place in London in 1979. But for the characters it is twenty-five years later.

ACT ONE

Scene One

Low bright sun. Verandah. Flagpole with union jack.
The family – CLIVE, BETTY, EDWARD,
VICTORIA, MAUD, ELLEN, JOSHUA

ALL (*sing*).   Come gather, sons of England, come gather in your
        pride.
        Now meet the world united, now face it side by
        side;
        Ye who the earth's wide corners, from veldt to
        prairie, roam.
        From bush and jungle muster all who call old
        England 'home'.
        Then gather round for England,
        Rally to the flag,
        From North and South and East and West
        Come one and all for England!

CLIVE.   This is my family. Though far from home
        We serve the Queen wherever we may roam.
        I am a father to the natives here,
        And father to my family so dear.

        He presents BETTY. *She is played by a man.*

        My wife is all I dreamt a wife should be,
        And everything she is she owes to me.

BETTY.   I live for Clive. The whole aim of my life
        Is to be what he looks for in a wife.
        I am a man's creation as you see,
        And what men want is what I want to be.

        CLIVE *presents* JOSHUA. *He is played by a white.*

CLIVE.   My boy's a jewel. Really has the knack.
        You'd hardly notice that the fellow's black.

JOSHUA.   My skin is black but oh my soul is white.
           I hate my tribe. My master is my light.
           I only live for him. As you can see,
           What white men want is what I want to be.

           CLIVE *presents* EDWARD. *He is played by a*
           woman.

CLIVE.   My son is young. I'm doing all I can
           To teach him to grow up to be a man.

EDWARD.   What father wants I'd dearly like to be.
           I find it rather hard as you can see.

           CLIVE *presents* VICTORIA, *who is a dummy,*
           MAUD, *and* ELLEN.

CLIVE.   No need for any speeches by the rest.
           My daughter, mother-in-law, and governess.

ALL (*sing*). O'er countless numbers she, our Queen,
           Victoria reigns supreme;
           O'er Afric's sunny plains, and o'er
           Canadian frozen stream;
           The forge of war shall weld the chains of
               brotherhood secure;
           So to all time in ev'ry clime our Empire shall
               endure.

           Then gather round for England,
           Rally to the flag,
           From North and South and East and West
           Come one and all for England!

           All go except BETTY. CLIVE *comes.*

BETTY.   Clive?

CLIVE.   Betty. Joshua!

           JOSHUA *comes with a drink for* CLIVE.

BETTY.   I thought you would never come. The day's so long
           without you.

CLIVE.   Long ride in the bush.

BETTY.   Is anything wrong? I heard drums.

CLIVE.   Nothing serious. Beauty is a damned good mare.
           I must get some new boots sent from home. These
           ones have never been right. I have a blister.

BETTY.   My poor dear foot.

CLIVE.   It's nothing.

BETTY.   Oh but it's sore.

CLIVE.   We are not in this country to enjoy ourselves.
           Must have ridden fifty miles. Spoke to three
           different headmen who would all gladly chop off
           each other's heads and wear them round their
           waists.

BETTY.   Clive!

CLIVE.   Don't be squeamish, Betty, let me have my
           joke. And what has my little dove done today?

BETTY.   I've read a little.

CLIVE.   Good. Is it good?

BETTY.   It's poetry.

CLIVE.   You're so delicate and sensitive.

BETTY.   And I played the piano. Shall I send for the
           children?

CLIVE.   Yes, in a minute. I've a piece of news for you.

BETTY.   Good news?

CLIVE.   You'll certainly think it's good. A visitor.

BETTY.   From home?

CLIVE.   No. Well of course originally from home.

BETTY.   Man or woman?

CLIVE.   Man.

BETTY.   I can't imagine.

CLIVE.   Something of an explorer. Bit of a poet. Odd
           chap but brave as a lion. And a great admirer of
           yours.

BETTY.   What do you mean? Whoever can it be?

CLIVE.   With an H and a B. And does conjuring tricks
           for little Edward.

BETTY.   That sounds like Mr Bagley.

CLIVE.   Harry Bagley.

BETTY.   He certainly doesn't admire me, Clive, what a thing to say. How could I possibly guess from that. He's hardly explored anything at all, he's just been up a river, he's done nothing at all compared to what you do. You should have said a heavy drinker and a bit of a bore.

CLIVE.   But you like him well enough. You don't mind him coming?

BETTY.   Anyone at all to break the monotony.

CLIVE.   But you have your mother. You have Ellen.

BETTY.   Ellen is a governess. My mother is my mother.

CLIVE.   I hoped when she came to visit she would be company for you.

BETTY.   I don't think mother is on a visit. I think she lives with us.

CLIVE.   I think she does.

BETTY.   Clive you are so good.

CLIVE.   But are you bored my love?

BETTY.   It's just that I miss you when you're away. We're not in this country to enjoy ourselves. If I lack society that is my form of service.

CLIVE.   That's a brave girl. So today has been all right? No fainting? No hysteria?

BETTY.   I have been very tranquil.

CLIVE.   Ah what a haven of peace to come home to. The coolth, the calm, the beauty.

BETTY.   There is one thing, Clive, if you don't mind.

CLIVE.   What can I do for you, my dear?

BETTY.   It's about Joshua.

CLIVE.   I wouldn't leave you alone here with a quiet mind if it weren't for Joshua.

BETTY.   Joshua doesn't like me.

CLIVE.   Joshua has been my boy for eight years. He has

saved my life. I have saved his life. He is devoted to me and to mine. I have said this before.

BETTY.   He is rude to me. He doesn't do what I say. Speak to him.

CLIVE.   Tell me what happened.

BETTY.   He said something improper.

CLIVE.   Well, what?

BETTY.   I don't like to repeat it.

CLIVE.   I must insist.

BETTY.   I had left my book inside on the piano. I was in the hammock. I asked him to fetch it.

CLIVE.   And did he not fetch it?

BETTY.   Yes, he did eventually.

CLIVE.   And what did he say?

BETTY.   Clive –

CLIVE.   Betty.

BETTY.   He said Fetch it yourself. You've got legs under that dress.

CLIVE.   Joshua!

JOSHUA *comes.*

Joshua, madam says you spoke impolitely to her this afternoon.

JOSHUA.   Sir?

CLIVE.   When she asked you to pass her book from the piano.

JOSHUA.   She has the book, sir.

BETTY.   I have the book now, but when I told you –

CLIVE.   Betty, please, let me handle this. You didn't pass it at once?

JOSHUA.   No sir, I made a joke first.

CLIVE.   What was that?

JOSHUA.	I said my legs were tired, sir. That was funny because the book was very near, it would not make my legs tired to get it.
BETTY.	That's not true.
JOSHUA.	Did madam hear me wrong?
CLIVE.	She heard something else.
JOSHUA.	What was that, madam?
BETTY.	Never mind.
CLIVE.	Now Joshua, it won't do you know. Madam doesn't like that kind of joke. You must do what madam says, just do what she says and don't answer back. You know your place, Joshua. I don't have to say any more.
JOSHUA.	No sir.
BETTY.	I expect an apology.
JOSHUA.	I apologise, madam.
CLIVE.	There now. It won't happen again, my dear. I'm very shocked Joshua, very shocked.

CLIVE *winks at* JOSHUA, *unseen by* BETTY. JOSHUA *goes.*

CLIVE.	I think another drink, and send for the children, and isn't that Harry riding down the hill? Wave, wave. Just in time before dark. Cuts it fine, the blighter. Always a hothead, Harry.
BETTY.	Can he see us?
CLIVE.	Stand further forward. He'll see your white dress. There, he waved back.
BETTY.	Do you think so? I wonder what he saw. Sometimes sunset is so terrifying I can't bear to look.
CLIVE.	It makes me proud. Elsewhere in the empire the sun is rising.
BETTY.	Harry looks so small on the hillside.

ELLEN *comes.*

ELLEN.   Shall I bring the children?

BETTY.   Shall Ellen bring the children?

CLIVE.   Delightful.

BETTY.   Yes, Ellen, make sure they're warm. The night
air is deceptive. Victoria was looking pale
yesterday.

CLIVE.   My love.

MAUD *comes from inside the house.*

MAUD.   Are you warm enough Betty?

BETTY.   Perfectly.

MAUD.   The night air is deceptive.

BETTY.   I'm quite warm. I'm too warm.

MAUD.   You're not getting a fever, I hope? She's not
strong, you know, Clive. I don't know how long
you'll keep her in this climate.

CLIVE.   I look after Her Majesty's domains. I think you
can trust me to look after my wife.

ELLEN *comes carrying* VICTORIA, *aged 2.*
EDWARD, *aged 9, lags behind.*

BETTY.   Victoria, my pet, say good evening to papa.

CLIVE *takes* VICTORIA *on his knee.*

CLIVE.   There's my sweet little Vicky. What have we
done today?

BETTY.   She wore Ellen's hat.

CLIVE.   Did she wear Ellen's big hat like a lady. What a
pretty.

BETTY.   And Joshua gave her a piggy back. Tell papa.
Horsy with Joshy?

ELLEN.   She's tired.

CLIVE.   Nice Joshy played horsy. What a big strong
Joshy. Did you have a gallop? Did you make him
stop and go? Not very chatty tonight are we?

BETTY.   Edward, say good evening to papa.

CLIVE.   Edward my boy. Have you done your lessons well?

EDWARD.   Yes papa.

CLIVE.   Did you go riding?

EDWARD.   Yes papa.

CLIVE.   What's that you're holding?

BETTY.   It's Victoria's doll. What are you doing with it, Edward?

EDWARD.   Minding her.

BETTY.   Well I should give it to Ellen quickly. You don't want papa to see you with a doll.

CLIVE.   No, we had you with Victoria's doll once before, Edward.

ELLEN.   He's minding it for Vicky. He's not playing with it.

BETTY.   He's not playing with it, Clive. He's minding it for Vicky.

CLIVE.   Ellen minds Victoria, let Ellen mind the doll.

ELLEN.   Come, give it to me.

            ELLEN *takes the doll.*

EDWARD.   Don't pull her about. Vicky's very fond of her. She likes me to have her.

BETTY.   He's a very good brother.

CLIVE.   Yes, it's manly of you Edward, to take care of your little sister. We'll say no more about it. Tomorrow I'll take you riding with me and Harry Bagley. Would you like that?

EDWARD.   Is he here?

CLIVE.   He's just arrived. There Betty, take Victoria now. I must go and welcome Harry.

            CLIVE *tosses* VICTORIA *to* BETTY, *who gives her to* ELLEN.

EDWARD.   Can I come, papa?

BETTY.   Is he warm enough?

EDWARD. Am I warm enough?

CLIVE. Never mind the women, Ned. Come and meet Harry.

They go. The women are left. There is a silence.

MAUD. I daresay Mr Bagley will be out all day and we'll see nothing of him.

BETTY. He plays the piano. Surely he will sometimes stay at home with us.

MAUD. We can't expect it. The men have their duties and we have ours.

BETTY. He won't have seen a piano for a year. He lives a very rough life.

ELLEN. Will it be exciting for you, Betty?

MAUD. Whatever do you mean, Ellen?

ELLEN. We don't have very much society.

BETTY. Clive is my society.

MAUD. It's time Victoria went to bed.

ELLEN. She'd like to stay up and see Mr Bagley.

MAUD. Mr Bagley can see her tomorrow.

ELLEN *goes.*

MAUD. You let that girl forget her place, Betty.

BETTY. Mother, she is governess to my son. I know what her place is. I think my friendship does her good. She is not very happy.

MAUD. Young women are never happy.

BETTY. Mother, what a thing to say.

MAUD. Then when they're older they look back and see that comparatively speaking they were ecstatic.

BETTY. I'm perfectly happy.

MAUD. You are looking very pretty tonight. You were such a success as a young girl. You have made a most fortunate marriage. I'm sure you will be an excellent hostess to Mr Bagley.

BETTY. I feel quite nervous at the thought of entertaining.

MAUD. I can always advise you if I'm asked.

BETTY. What a long time they're taking. I always seem to be waiting for the men.

MAUD. Betty you have to learn to be patient. I am patient. My mama was very patient.

CLIVE approaches, supporting CAROLINE SAUNDERS.

CLIVE. It is a pleasure. It is an honour. It is positively your duty to seek my help. I would be hurt, I would be insulted by any show of independence. Your husband would have been one of my dearest friends if he had lived. Betty, look who has come, Mrs Saunders. She has ridden here all alone, amazing spirit. What will you have? Tea or something stronger? Let her lie down, she is overcome. Betty, you will know what to do.

MRS SAUNDERS *lies down.*

MAUD. I knew it. I heard drums. We'll be killed in our beds.

CLIVE. Now, please, calm yourself.

MAUD. I am perfectly calm. I am just outspoken. If it comes to being killed I shall take it as calmly as anyone.

CLIVE. There is no cause for alarm. Mrs Saunders has been alone since her husband died last year, amazing spirit. Not surprisingly, the strain has told. She has come to us as her nearest neighbours.

MAUD. What happened to make her come?

CLIVE. This is not an easy country for a woman.

MAUD. Clive, I heard drums. We are not children.

CLIVE. Of course you heard drums. The tribes are constantly at war, if the term is not too grand to grace their squabbles. Not unnaturally Mrs

Saunders would like the company of white
women. The piano. Poetry.

BETTY.   We are not her nearest neighbours.

CLIVE.   We are among her nearest neighbours and I was
a dear friend of her late husband. She knows
that she will find a welcome here. She will not be
disappointed. She will be cared for.

MAUD.   Of course we will care for her.

BETTY.   Victoria is in bed. I must go and say goodnight.
Mother, please, you look after Mrs Saunders.

CLIVE.   Harry will be here at once.

           BETTY *goes*.

MAUD.   How rash to go out after dark without a shawl.

CLIVE.   Amazing spirit. Drink this.

MRS SAUNDERS. Where am I?

MAUD.   You are quite safe.

MRS SAUNDERS. Clive? Clive? Thank God. This is very
kind. How do you do? I am sorry to be a
nuisance. Charmed. Have you a gun? I have a
gun.

CLIVE.   There is no need for guns I hope. We are all
friends here.

MRS SAUNDERS. I think I will lie down again.

           HARRY BAGLEY *and* EDWARD *have approached*.

MAUD.   Ah, here is Mr Bagley.

EDWARD.   I gave his horse some water.

CLIVE.   You don't know Mrs Saunders, do you Harry?
She has at present collapsed, but she is
recovering thanks to the good offices of my
wife's mother who I think you've met before.
Betty will be along in a minute. Edward will go
home to school shortly. He is quite a young man
since you saw him.

HARRY.   I hardly knew him.

MAUD.   What news have you for us, Mr Bagley?

CLIVE.   Do you know Mrs Saunders, Harry? Amazing spirit.

EDWARD.   Did you hardly know me?

HARRY.   Of course I knew you. I mean you have grown.

EDWARD.   What do you expect?

HARRY.   That's quite right, people don't get smaller.

MAUD.   Edward. You should be in bed.

EDWARD.   No, I'm not tired, I'm not tired am I Uncle Harry?

HARRY.   I don't think he's tired.

CLIVE.   He is overtired. It is past his bedtime. Say goodnight.

EDWARD.   Goodnight, sir.

CLIVE.   And to your grandmother.

EDWARD.   Goodnight, grandmother.

            EDWARD *goes*.

MAUD.   Shall I help Mrs Saunders indoors? I'm afraid she may get a chill.

CLIVE.   Shall I give her an arm?

MAUD.   How kind of you Clive. I think I am strong enough.

            MAUD *helps* MRS SAUNDERS *into the house*.

CLIVE.   Not a word to alarm the women.

HARRY.   Absolutely.

CLIVE.   I did some good today I think. Kept up some alliances. There's a lot of affection there.

HARRY.   They're affectionate people. They can be very cruel of course.

CLIVE.   Well they are savages.

HARRY.   Very beautiful people many of them.

CLIVE.   Joshua! (*To* HARRY.) I think we should sleep
          with guns.

HARRY.   I haven't slept in a house for six months. It
          seems extremely safe.

          JOSHUA *comes.*

CLIVE.   Joshua, you will have gathered there's a spot of
          bother. Rumours of this and that. You should be
          armed I think.

JOSHUA.   There are many bad men, sir. I pray about it.
          Jesus will protect us.

CLIVE.   He will indeed and I'll also get you a weapon.
          Betty, come and keep Harry company. Look in
          the barn, Joshua, every night.

          CLIVE *and* JOSHUA *go.* BETTY *comes.*

HARRY.   I wondered where you were.

BETTY.   I was singing lullabies.

HARRY.   When I think of you I always think of you with
          Edward in your lap.

BETTY.   Do you think of me sometimes then?

HARRY.   You have been thought of where no white
          woman has ever been thought of before.

BETTY.   It's one way of having adventures. I suppose
          I will never go in person.

HARRY.   That's up to you.

BETTY.   Of course it's not. I have duties.

HARRY.   Are you happy, Betty?

BETTY.   Where have you been?

HARRY.   Built a raft and went up the river. Stayed with
          some people. The king is always very good to me.
          They have a lot of skulls around the place but
          not white men's I think. I made up a poem one
          night. If I should die in this forsaken spot, There
          is a loving heart without a blot, Where I will
          live – and so on.

BETTY.   When I'm near you it's like going out into the
           jungle. It's like going up the river on a raft.
           It's like going out in the dark.

HARRY.   And you are safety and light and peace and
           home.

BETTY.   But I want to be dangerous.

HARRY.   Clive is my friend.

BETTY.   I am your friend.

HARRY.   I don't like dangerous women.

BETTY.   Is Mrs Saunders dangerous?

HARRY.   Not to me. She's a bit of an old boot.

           JOSHUA *comes, unobserved.*

BETTY.   Am I dangerous?

HARRY.   You are rather.

BETTY.   Please like me.

HARRY.   I worship you.

BETTY.   Please want me.

HARRY.   I don't want to want you. Of course I want you.

BETTY.   What are we going to do?

HARRY.   I should have stayed on the river. The hell
           with it.

           *He goes to take her in his arms, she runs away into
           the house.* HARRY *stays where he is. He becomes
           aware of* JOSHUA.

HARRY.   Who's there?

JOSHUA.   Only me sir.

HARRY.   Got a gun now have you?

JOSHUA.   Yes sir.

HARRY.   Where's Clive?

JOSHUA.   Going round the boundaries sir.

HARRY.   Have you checked there's nobody in the barns?

JOSHUA. Yes sir.

HARRY. Shall we go in a barn and fuck? It's not an order.

JOSHUA. That's all right, yes.

They go off.

Scene Two

An open space some distance from the house.
MRS SAUNDERS *alone, breathless. She is*
carrying a riding crop. CLIVE *arrives.*

CLIVE. Why? Why?

MRS SAUNDERS. Don't fuss, Clive, it makes you sweat.

CLIVE. Why ride off now? Sweat, you would sweat if you were in love with somebody as disgustingly capricious as you are. You will be shot with poisoned arrows. You will miss the picnic. Somebody will notice I came after you.

MRS SAUNDERS. I didn't want you to come after me. I wanted to be alone.

CLIVE. You will be raped by cannibals.

MRS SAUNDERS. I just wanted to get out of your house.

CLIVE. My God, what women put us through. Cruel, cruel. I think you are the sort of woman who would enjoy whipping somebody. I've never met one before.

MRS SAUNDERS. Can I tell you something, Clive?

CLIVE. Let me tell you something first. Since you came to the house I have had an erection twenty-four hours a day except for ten minutes after the time we had intercourse.

MRS SAUNDERS. I don't think that's physically possible.

CLIVE. You are causing me appalling physical suffering. Is this the way to treat a benefactor?

MRS SAUNDERS. Clive, when I came to your house the other night I came because I was afraid. The cook was going to let his whole tribe in through the window.

CLIVE.   I know that, my poor sweet. Amazing –

MRS SAUNDERS. I came to you although you are not my nearest neighbour –

CLIVE.   Rather than to the old major of seventy-two.

MRS SAUNDERS. Because the last time he came to visit me I had to defend myself with a shotgun and I thought you would take no for an answer.

CLIVE.   But you've already answered yes.

MRS SAUNDERS. I answered yes once. Sometimes I want to say no.

CLIVE.   Women, my God. Look the picnic will start, I have to go to the picnic. Please Caroline

MRS SAUNDERS. I think I will have to go back to my own house.

CLIVE.   Caroline, if you were shot with poisoned arrows do you know what I'd do? I'd fuck your dead body and poison myself. Caroline, you smell amazing. You terrify me. You are dark like this continent. Mysterious. Treacherous. When you rode to me through the night. When you fainted in my arms. When I came to you in your bed, when I lifted the mosquito netting, when I said let me in, let me in. Oh don't shut me out, Caroline, let me in.

He has been caressing her feet and legs. He disappears completely under her skirt.

MRS SAUNDERS. Please stop. I can't concentrate. I want to go home. I wish I didn't enjoy the sensation because I don't like you, Clive. I do like living in your house where there's plenty of guns. But I don't like you at all. But I do like the sensation. Well I'll have it then. I'll have it, I'll have it –

Voices are heard singing The First Noël.

Don't stop. Don't stop.

CLIVE *comes out from under her skirt.*

CLIVE.   The Christmas picnic. I came.

MRS SAUNDERS. I didn't.

CLIVE.   I'm all sticky.

MRS SAUNDERS. What about me? Wait.

CLIVE.   All right, are you? Come on. We mustn't be found.

MRS SAUNDERS. Don't go now.

CLIVE.   Caroline, you are so voracious. Do let go. Tidy yourself up. There's a hair in my mouth.

CLIVE *and* MRS SAUNDERS *go off.* BETTY *and* MAUD *come, with* JOSHUA *carrying hamper.*

MAUD.   I never would have thought a guinea fowl could taste so like a turkey.

BETTY.   I had to explain to Cook three times.

MAUD.   You did very well dear.

JOSHUA *sits apart with gun.* EDWARD *and* HARRY *with* VICTORIA *on his shoulder, singing The First Noël.* MAUD *and* BETTY *are unpacking the hamper.* CLIVE *arrives separately.*

MAUD.   This tablecloth was one of my mama's.

BETTY.   Uncle Harry playing horsy.

EDWARD.   Crackers crackers.

BETTY.   Not yet, Edward.

CLIVE.   And now the moment we have all been waiting for.

CLIVE *opens champagne. General acclaim.*

CLIVE.   Oh dear, stained my trousers, never mind.

EDWARD.   Can I have some?

MAUD.   Oh no Edward, not for you.

CLIVE.   Give him half a glass.

MAUD.   If your father says so.

CLIVE.   All rise please. To Her Majesty Queen Victoria,
           God bless her, and her husband and all her dear
           children.

ALL.   The Queen.

EDWARD.   Crackers crackers.

           General cracker pulling, hats. CLIVE *and* HARRY
           discuss champagne.

HARRY.   Excellent, Clive, wherever did you get it?

CLIVE.   I know a chap in French Equatorial Africa.

EDWARD.   I won, I won mama.

           ELLEN *arrives.*

BETTY.   Give a hat to Joshua, he'd like it.

           EDWARD *takes hat to* JOSHUA. BETTY *takes
           a ball from the hamper and plays catch with*
           ELLEN. *Murmurs of surprise and congratulation
           from the men as they catch the ball.*

EDWARD.   Mama, don't play. You know you can't catch
           a ball.

BETTY.   He's perfectly right. I can't throw either.

           BETTY *sits down.* ELLEN *has the ball.*

EDWARD.   Ellen, don't you play either. You're no good.
           You spoil it.

           EDWARD *takes* VICTORIA *from* HARRY *and
           gives her to* ELLEN. *He takes the ball and
           throws it to* HARRY. HARRY, CLIVE *and*
           EDWARD *play ball.*

BETTY.   Ellen come and sit with me. We'll be spectators
           and clap.

           EDWARD *misses the ball.*

CLIVE.   Butterfingers.

EDWARD.   I'm not.

HARRY.   Throw straight now.

EDWARD.   I did, I did.

CLIVE.   Keep your eye on the ball.

EDWARD.   You can't throw.

CLIVE.   Don't be a baby.

EDWARD.   I'm not, throw a hard one, throw a hard one –

CLIVE.   Butterfingers. What will Uncle Harry think of you?

EDWARD.   It's your fault. You can't throw. I hate you.

He throws the ball wildly in the direction of JOSHUA.

CLIVE.   Now you've lost the ball. He's lost the ball.

EDWARD.   It's Joshua's fault. Joshua's butterfingers.

CLIVE.   I don't think I want to play any more. Joshua, find the ball will you?

EDWARD.   Yes, please play. I'll find the ball. Please play.

CLIVE.   You're so silly and you can't catch. You'll be no good at cricket.

MAUD.   Why don't we play hide and seck?

EDWARD.   Because it's a baby game.

BETTY.   You've hurt Edward's feelings.

CLIVE.   A boy has no business having feelings.

HARRY.   Hide and seek. I'll be it. Everybody must hide. This is the base, you have to get home to base.

EDWARD.   Hide and seek, hide and seek.

HARRY.   Can we persuade the ladies to join us?

MAUD.   I'm playing. I love games.

BETTY.   I always get found straight away.

ELLEN.   Come on, Betty, do. Vicky wants to play.

EDWARD.   You won't find me ever.

They all go except CLIVE, HARRY, JOSHUA.

HARRY. It is safe, I suppose?

CLIVE. They won't go far. This is very much my territory and it's broad daylight. Joshua will keep an open eye.

HARRY. Well I must give them a hundred. You don't know what this means to me, Clive. A chap can only go on so long alone. I can climb mountains and go down rivers, but what's it for? For Christmas and England and games and women singing. This is the empire, Clive. It's not me putting a flag in new lands. It's you. The empire is one big family. I'm one of its black sheep, Clive. And I know you think my life is rather dashing. But I want you to know I admire you. This is the empire, Clive, and I serve it. With all my heart.

CLIVE. I think that's about a hundred.

HARRY. Ready or not, here I come!

He goes.

CLIVE. Harry Bagley is a fine man, Joshua. You should be proud to know him. He will be in history books.

JOSHUA. Sir, while we are alone.

CLIVE. Joshua of course, what is it? You always have my ear. Any time.

JOSHUA. Sir, I have some information. The stable boys are not to be trusted. They whisper. They go out at night. They visit their people. Their people are not my people. I do not visit my people.

CLIVE. Thank you, Joshua. They certainly look after Beauty. I'll be sorry to have to replace them.

JOSHUA. They carry knives.

CLIVE. Thank you, Joshua.

JOSHUA. And, sir.

CLIVE. I appreciate this, Joshua, very much.

JOSHUA.   Your wife.

CLIVE.   Ah, yes?

JOSHUA.   She also thinks Harry Bagley is a fine man.

CLIVE.   Thank you, Joshua.

JOSHUA.   Are you going to hide?

CLIVE.   Yes, yes I am. Thank you. Keep your eyes open
Joshua.

JOSHUA.   I do, sir.

CLIVE *goes.* JOSHUA *goes.* HARRY *and* BETTY
race back to base.

BETTY.   I can't run, I can't run at all.

HARRY.   There, I've caught you.

BETTY.   Harry, what are we going to do?

HARRY.   It's impossible, Betty.

BETTY.   Shall we run away together?

MAUD *comes.*

MAUD.   I give up. Don't catch me. I have been stung.

HARRY.   Nothing serious I hope.

MAUD.   I have ointment in my bag. I always carry
ointment. I shall just sit down and rest. I am too
old for all this fun. Hadn't you better be seeking,
Harry?

HARRY *goes.* MAUD *and* BETTY *are alone for
some time. They don't speak.* HARRY *and* EDWARD
race back.

EDWARD.   I won, I won, you didn't catch me.

HARRY.   Yes I did.

EDWARD.   Mama, who was first?

BETTY.   I wasn't watching. I think it was Harry.

EDWARD.   It wasn't Harry. You're no good at judging.
I won, didn't I grandma?

MAUD.   I expect so, since it's Christmas.

EDWARD.   I won, Uncle Harry. I'm better than you.

BETTY.   Why don't you help Uncle Harry look for the
           others?

EDWARD.   Shall I?

HARRY.   Yes, of course.

BETTY.   Run along then. He's just coming.

           EDWARD *goes.*

           Harry, I shall scream.

HARRY.   Ready or not here I come.

           HARRY *runs off.*

BETTY.   Why don't you go back to the house, mother,
           and rest your insect-bite?

MAUD.   Betty, my duty is here. I don't like what I see
           Clive wouldn't like it, Betty. I am your mother.

BETTY.   Clive gives you a home because you are my
           mother.

           HARRY *comes back.*

HARRY.   I can't find anyone else. I'm getting quite hot.

BETTY.   Sit down a minute.

HARRY.   I can't do that. I'm he. How's your sting?

MAUD.   It seems to be swelling up.

BETTY.   Why don't you go home and rest? Joshua will go
           with you. Joshua!

HARRY.   I could take you back.

MAUD.   That would be charming.

BETTY.   You can't go. You're he.

           JOSHUA *comes.*

BETTY.   Joshua, my mother wants to go back to the
           house. Will you go with her please.

JOSHUA.   Sir told me I have to keep an eye.

BETTY.   I am telling you to go back to the house. Then you can come back here and keep an eye.

MAUD.   Thank you Betty. I know we have our little differences, but I always want what is best for you.

JOSHUA and MAUD go.

HARRY.   Don't give way. Keep calm.

BETTY.   I shall kill myself.

HARRY.   Betty, you are a star in my sky. Without you I would have no sense of direction. I need you, and I need you where you are, I need you to be Clive's wife. I need to go up rivers and know you are sitting here thinking of me.

BETTY.   I want more than that. Is that wicked of me?

HARRY.   Not wicked, Betty. Silly.

EDWARD calls in the distance.

EDWARD.   Uncle Harry, where are you?

BETTY.   Can't we ever be alone?

HARRY.   You are a mother. And a daughter. And a wife.

BETTY.   I think I shall go and hide again.

BETTY goes. HARRY goes. CLIVE chases MRS SAUNDERS across the stage. EDWARD and HARRY call in the distance.

EDWARD.   Uncle Harry!

HARRY.   Edward!

EDWARD comes.

EDWARD.   Uncle Harry!

HARRY comes.

There you are. I haven't found anyone have you?

HARRY.   I wonder where they all are.

EDWARD.   Perhaps they're lost forever. Perhaps they're dead. There's trouble going on isn't there, and

	nobody says because of not frightening the women and children.
HARRY.	Yes, that's right.
EDWARD.	Do you think we'll be killed in our beds?
HARRY.	Not very likely.
EDWARD.	I can't sleep at night. Can you?
HARRY.	I'm not used to sleeping in a house.
EDWARD.	If I'm awake at night can I come and see you? I won't wake you up. I'll only come in if you're awake.
HARRY.	You should try to sleep.
EDWARD.	I don't mind being awake because I make up adventures. Once we were on a raft going down to the rapids. We've lost the paddles because we used them to fight off the crocodiles. A crocodile comes at me and I stab it again and again and the blood is everywhere and it tips up the raft and it has you by the leg and it's biting your leg right off and I take my knife and stab it in the throat and rip open its stomach and it lets go of you but it bites my hand but it's dead. And I drag you onto the river bank and I'm almost fainting with pain and we lie there in each other's arms.
HARRY.	Have I lost my leg?
EDWARD.	I forgot about the leg by then.
HARRY.	Hadn't we better look for the others?
EDWARD.	Wait. I've got something for you. It was in mama's box but she never wears it.

EDWARD gives HARRY a necklace.

You don't have to wear it either but you might like it to look at.

HARRY.	It's beautiful. But you'll have to put it back.
EDWARD.	I wanted to give it to you.
HARRY.	You did. It can go back in the box. You still gave

it to me. Come on now, we have to find the
others.

EDWARD.   Harry, I love you.

HARRY.   Yes I know. I love you too.

EDWARD.   You know what we did when you were here
before. I want to do it again. I think about it all
the time. I try to do it to myself but it's not as
good. Don't you want to any more?

HARRY.   I do, but it's a sin and a crime and it's also
wrong.

EDWARD.   But we'll do it anyway won't we?

HARRY.   Yes of course.

EDWARD.   I wish the others would all be killed. Take it out
now and let me see it.

HARRY.   No.

EDWARD.   Is it big now?

HARRY.   Yes.

EDWARD.   Let me touch it.

HARRY.   No.

EDWARD.   Just hold me.

HARRY.   When you can't sleep.

EDWARD.   We'd better find the others then. Come on.

HARRY.   Ready or not, here we come.

They go out with whoops and shouts. BETTY *and*
ELLEN *come.*

BETTY.   Ellen, I don't want to play any more.

ELLEN.   Nor do I, Betty.

BETTY.   Come and sit here with me. Oh Ellen, what will
become of me?

ELLEN.   Betty, are you crying? Are you laughing?

BETTY.   Tell me what you think of Harry Bagley.

ELLEN.   He's a very fine man.

BETTY.   No, Ellen, what you really think.

ELLEN.   I think you think he's very handsome.

BETTY.   And don't you think he is? Oh Ellen, you're so good and I'm so wicked.

ELLEN.   I'm not so good as you think.

EDWARD *comes.*

EDWARD.   I've found you.

ELLEN.   We're not hiding Edward.

EDWARD.   But I found you.

ELLEN.   We're not playing, Edward, now run along.

EDWARD.   Come on, Ellen, do play. Come on, mama.

ELLEN.   Edward, don't pull your mama like that.

BETTY.   Edward, you must do what your governess says. Go and play with Uncle Harry.

EDWARD.   Uncle Harry!

EDWARD *goes.*

BETTY.   Ellen, can you keep a secret?

ELLEN.   Oh yes, yes please.

BETTY.   I love Harry Bagley. I want to go away with him. There, I've said it, it's true.

ELLEN.   How do you know you love him?

BETTY.   I kissed him.

ELLEN.   Betty.

BETTY.   He held my hand like this. Oh I want him to do it again. I want him to stroke my hair.

ELLEN.   Your lovely hair. Like this, Betty?

BETTY.   I want him to put his arm around my waist.

ELLEN.   Like this, Betty?

BETTY.   Yes, oh I want him to kiss me again.

ELLEN.   Like this Betty?

ELLEN kisses BETTY.

BETTY.	Ellen, whatever are you doing? It's not a joke.
ELLEN.	I'm sorry, Betty. You're so pretty. Harry Bagley doesn't deserve you. You wouldn't really go away with him?
BETTY.	Oh Ellen, you don't know what I suffer. You don't know what love is. Everyone will hate me, but it's worth it for Harry's love.
ELLEN.	I don't hate you, Betty, I love you.
BETTY.	Harry says we shouldn't go away. But he says he worships me.
ELLEN.	I worship you Betty.
BETTY.	Oh Ellen, you are my only friend.

They embrace. The others have all gathered together. MAUD *has rejoined the party, and* JOSHUA.

CLIVE.	Come along everyone, you mustn't miss Harry's conjuring trick.

BETTY *and* ELLEN *go to join the others.*

MAUD.	I didn't want to spoil the fun by not being here.
HARRY.	What is it that flies all over the world and is up my sleeve?

HARRY *produces a union jack from up his sleeve. General acclaim.*

CLIVE.	I think we should have some singing now. Ladies, I rely on you to lead the way.
ELLEN.	We have a surprise for you. I have taught Joshua a Christmas carol. He has been singing it at the piano but I'm sure he can sing it unaccompanied, can't you, Joshua?
JOSHUA.	In the deep midwinter Frosty wind made moan, Earth stood hard as iron, Water like a stone. Snow had fallen snow on snow

> Snow on snow,
> In the deep midwinter
> Long long ago.

> What can I give him
> Poor as I am?
> If I were a shepherd
> I would bring a lamb.
> If I were a wise man
> I would do my part.
> What I can I give him?
> Give my heart.

Scene Three

Inside the house. BETTY, MRS SAUNDERS,
MAUD *with* VICTORIA. *The blinds are down so the
light isn't bright though it is day outside.* CLIVE
looks in.

CLIVE.   Everything all right? Nothing to be frightened of.

   CLIVE *goes. Silence.*

MAUD.   Clap hands, daddy comes, with his pockets full
   of plums. All for Vicky.

   Silence.

MRS SAUNDERS. Who actually does the flogging?

MAUD.   I don't think we want to imagine.

MRS SAUNDERS. I imagine Joshua.

BETTY.   Yes I think it would be Joshua. Or would Clive
   do it himself?

MRS SAUNDERS. Well we can ask them afterwards.

MAUD.   I don't like the way you speak of it, Mrs
   Saunders.

MRS SAUNDERS. How should I speak of it?

MAUD.   The men will do it in the proper way, whatever it
   is. We have our own part to play.

MRS SAUNDERS. Harry Bagley says they should just be sent away. I don't think he likes to see them beaten.

BETTY.   Harry is so tender hearted. Perhaps he is right.

MAUD.   Harry Bagley is not altogether – He has lived in this country a long time without any responsibilities. It is part of his charm but it hasn't improved his judgment. If the boys were just sent away they would go back to the village and make more trouble.

MRS SAUNDERS. And what will they say about us in the village if they've been flogged?

BETTY.   Perhaps Clive should keep them here.

MRS SAUNDERS. That is never wise.

BETTY.   Whatever shall we do?

MAUD.   I don't think it is up to us to wonder. The men don't tell us what is going on among the tribes, so how can we possibly make a judgment?

MRS SAUNDERS. I know a little of what is going on.

BETTY.   Tell me what you know. Clive tells me nothing.

MAUD.   You would not want to be told about it, Betty. It is enough for you that Clive knows what is happening. Clive will know what to do. Your father always knew what to do.

BETTY.   Are you saying you would do something different, Caroline?

MRS SAUNDERS. I would do what I did at my own home. I left. I can't see any way out except to leave. I will leave here. I will keep leaving everywhere I suppose.

MAUD.   Luckily this household has a head. I am squeamish myself. But luckily Clive is not.

BETTY.   You are leaving here then, Caroline?

MRS SAUNDERS. Not immediately. I'm sorry.

> *Silence.*

MRS SAUNDERS. I wonder if it's over.

>EDWARD *comes in.*

BETTY.   Shouldn't you be with the men, Edward?

EDWARD. I didn't want to see any more. They got what they deserved. Uncle Harry said I could come in.

MRS SAUNDERS. I never allowed the servants to be beaten in my own house. I'm going to find out what's happening.

>MRS SAUNDERS *goes out.*

BETTY.   Will she go and look?

MAUD.   Let Mrs Saunders be a warning to you, Betty. She is alone in the world. You are not, thank God. Since your father died, I know what it is to be unprotected. Vicky is such a pretty little girl. Clap hands, daddy comes, with his pockets full of plums. All for Vicky.

>EDWARD, *meanwhile, has found the doll and is playing clap hands with her.*

BETTY.   Edward, what have you got there?

EDWARD. I'm minding her.

BETTY.   Edward, I've told you before, dolls are for girls.

MAUD.   Where is Ellen? She should be looking after Edward. *(She goes to the door.)* Ellen! Betty, why do you let that girl mope about in her own room? That's not what she's come to Africa for.

BETTY.   You must never let the boys at school know you like dolls. Never, never. No one will talk to you, you won't be on the cricket team, you won't grow up to be a man like your papa.

EDWARD. I don't want to be like papa. I hate papa.

MAUD.   Edward! Edward!

BETTY.   You're a horrid wicked boy and papa will beat you. Of course you don't hate him, you love him. Now give Victoria her doll at once.

EDWARD. She's not Victoria's doll, she's my doll. She

doesn't love Victoria and Victoria doesn't love her. Victoria never even plays with her.

MAUD. Victoria will learn to play with her.

EDWARD. She's mine and she loves me and she won't be happy if you take her away, she'll cry, she'll cry, she'll cry.

BETTY takes the doll away, slaps him, bursts into tears. ELLEN comes in.

BETTY. Ellen, look what you've done. Edward's got the doll again. Now, Ellen, will you please do your job.

ELLEN. Edward, you are a wicked boy. I am going to lock you in the nursery until supper time. Now go upstairs this minute.

She slaps EDWARD, who bursts into tears and goes out.

I do try to do what you want. I'm so sorry.

ELLEN bursts into tears and goes out.

MAUD. There now, Vicky's got her baby back. Where did Vicky's naughty baby go? Shall we smack her? Just a little smack. (MAUD *smacks the doll hard.*) There, now she's a good baby. Clap hands, daddy comes, with his pockets full of plums. All for Vicky's baby. When I was a child we honoured our parents. My mama was an angel.

JOSHUA comes in. He stands without speaking.

BETTY. Joshua?

JOSHUA. Madam?

BETTY. Did you want something?

JOSHUA. Sent to see the ladies are all right, madam.

MRS SAUNDERS comes in.

MRS SAUNDERS. We're very well thank you, Joshua, and how are you?

JOSHUA. Very well thank you, Mrs Saunders.

MRS SAUNDERS. And the stable boys?

JOSHUA.   They have had justice, madam.

MRS SAUNDERS. So I saw. And does your arm ache?

MAUD.   This is not a proper conversation, Mrs Saunders.

MRS SAUNDERS. You don't mind beating your own people?

JOSHUA.   Not my people, madam.

MRS SAUNDERS. A different tribe?

JOSHUA.   Bad people.

HARRY and CLIVE come in.

CLIVE.   Well this is all very gloomy and solemn. Can we have the shutters open? The heat of the day has gone, we could have some light, I think. And cool drinks on the verandah, Joshua. Have some lemonade yourself. It is most refreshing.

Sunlight floods in as the shutters are opened.
EDWARD comes.

EDWARD.   Papa, papa, Ellen tried to lock me in the nursery. Mama is going to tell you of me. I'd rather tell you myself. I was playing with Vicky's doll again and I know it's very bad of me. And I said I didn't want to be like you and I said I hated you. And it's not true and I'm sorry, I'm sorry and please beat me and forgive me.

CLIVE.   Well there's a brave boy to own up. You should always respect and love me, Edward, not for myself, I may not deserve it, but as I respected and loved my own father, because he was my father. Through our father we love our Queen and our God, Edward. Do you understand? It is something men understand.

EDWARD.   Yes papa.

CLIVE.   Then I forgive you and shake you by the hand. You spend too much time with the women. You may spend more time with me and Uncle Harry, little man.

EDWARD.   I don't like women. I don't like dolls. I love you, papa, and I love you, Uncle Harry.

CLIVE.   There's a fine fellow. Let us go out onto the verandah.

They all start to go. EDWARD *takes* HARRY's *hand and goes with him.* CLIVE *draws* BETTY *back. They embrace.*

BETTY.   Poor Clive.

CLIVE.   It was my duty to have them flogged. For you and Edward and Victoria, to keep you safe.

BETTY.   It is terrible to feel betrayed.

CLIVE.   You can tame a wild animal only so far. They revert to their true nature and savage your hand. Sometimes I feel the natives are the enemy. I know that is wrong. I know I have a responsibility towards them, to care for them and bring them all to be like Joshua. But there is something dangerous. Implacable. This whole continent is my enemy. I am pitching my whole mind and will and reason and spirit against it to tame it, and I sometimes feel it will break over me and swallow me up.

BETTY.   Clive, Clive, I am here. I have faith in you.

CLIVE.   Yes, I can show you my moments of weakness, Betty, because you are my wife and because I trust you. I trust you, Betty, and it would break my heart if you did not deserve that trust. Harry Bagley is my friend. It would break my heart if he did not deserve my trust.

BETTY.   I'm sorry, I'm sorry. Forgive me. It is not Harry's fault, it is all mine. Harry is noble. He has rejected me. It is my wickedness. I get bored, I get restless, I imagine things. There is something so wicked in me, Clive.

CLIVE.   I have never thought of you having the weakness of your sex, only the good qualities.

BETTY.   I am bad, bad, bad –

CLIVE.   You are thoughtless, Betty, that's all. Women can be treacherous and evil. They are darker and more dangerous than men. The family protects us from that, you protect me from that. You are not that sort of woman. You are not unfaithful to me, Betty. I can't believe you are. It would hurt me so much to cast you off. That would be my duty.

BETTY.   No, no, no.

CLIVE.   Joshua has seen you kissing.

BETTY.   Forgive me.

CLIVE.   But I don't want to know about it. I don't want to know. I wonder of course, I wonder constantly. If Harry Bagley was not my friend I would shoot him. If I shot you every British man and woman would applaud me. But no. It was a moment of passion such as women are too weak to resist. But you must resist it, Betty, or it will destroy us. We must fight against it. We must resist this dark female lust, Betty, or it will swallow us up.

BETTY.   I do, I do resist. Help me. Forgive me.

CLIVE.   Yes I do forgive you. But I can't feel the same about you as I did. You are still my wife and we still have duties to the household.

They go out arm in arm. As soon as they have gone EDWARD sneaks back to get the doll, which has been dropped on the floor. He picks it up and comforts it. JOSHUA comes through with a tray of drinks.

JOSHUA.   Baby. Sissy. Girly.

JOSHUA goes. BETTY calls from off.

BETTY.   Edward?

BETTY comes in.

BETTY.   There you are my darling. Come, papa wants us all to be together. Uncle Harry is going to tell how he caught a crocodile. Mama's sorry she smacked you.

They embrace. JOSHUA *comes in again, passing through.*

BETTY.   Joshua, fetch me some blue thread from my sewing box. It is on the piano.

JOSHUA.   You've got legs under that skirt.

BETTY.   Joshua.

JOSHUA.   And more than legs.

BETTY.   Edward, are you going to stand there and let a servant insult your mother?

EDWARD.   Joshua, get my mother's thread.

JOSHUA.   Oh little Eddy, playing at master. It's only a joke.

EDWARD.   Don't speak to my mother like that again.

JOSHUA.   Ladies have no sense of humour. You like a joke with Joshua.

EDWARD.   You fetch her sewing at once, do you hear me? You move when I speak to you, boy.

JOSHUA.   Yes sir, master Edward sir.

           JOSHUA *goes.*

BETTY.   Edward, you were wonderful.

           She goes to embrace him but he moves away.

EDWARD.   Don't touch me.

ALL (*sing 'A Boys Best Friend'*).
           While plodding on our way, the toilsome road of
               life,
           How few the friends that daily there we meet.
           Not many will stand by in trouble and in
               strife,
           With counsel and affection ever sweet.
           But there is one whose smile will ever on us
               beam,
           Whose love is dearer far than any other;
           And wherever we may turn
           This lesson we will learn
           A boy's best friend is his mother.

> Then cherish her with care
> And smooth her silv'ry hair,
> When gone you will never get another.
> And wherever we may turn
> This lesson we shall learn,
> A boy's best friend is his mother.

Scene Four

The verandah as in Scene One. Early morning. Nobody there. JOSHUA comes out of the house slowly and stands for some time doing nothing. EDWARD comes out.

EDWARD.   Tell me another bad story, Joshua. Nobody else is even awake yet.

JOSHUA.   First there was nothing and then there was the great goddess. She was very large and she had golden eyes and she made the stars and the sun and the earth. But soon she was miserable and lonely and she cried like a great waterfall and her tears made all the rivers in the world. So the great spirit sent a terrible monster, a tree with hundreds of eyes and a long green tongue, and it came chasing after her and she jumped into a lake and the tree jumped in after her, and she jumped right up into the sky. And the tree couldn't follow, he was stuck in the mud. So he picked up a big handful of mud and he threw it at her, up among the stars, and it hit her on the head. And she fell down onto the earth into his arms and the ball of mud is the moon in the sky. And then they had children which is all of us.

EDWARD.   It's not true, though.

JOSHUA.   Of course it's not true. It's a bad story. Adam and Eve is true. God made man white like him and gave him the bad woman who liked the snake and gave us all this trouble.

CLIVE *and* HARRY *come out.*

CLIVE. Run along now, Edward. No, you may stay. You mustn't repeat anything you hear to your mother or your grandmother or Ellen.

EDWARD. Or Mrs Saunders?

CLIVE. Mrs Saunders is an unusual woman and does not require protection in the same way. Harry, there was trouble last night where we expected it. But it's all over now. Everything is under control but nobody should leave the house today I think.

HARRY. Casualties?

CLIVE. No, none of the soldiers hurt thank God. We did a certain amount of damage, set a village on fire and so forth.

HARRY. Was that necessary?

CLIVE. Obviously, it was necessary, Harry, or it wouldn't have happened. The army will come and visit, no doubt. You'll like that, eh, Joshua, to see the British army? And a treat for you, Edward, to see the soldiers. Would you like to be a soldier?

EDWARD. I'd rather be an explorer.

CLIVE. Ah, Harry, like you, you see. I didn't know an explorer at his age. Breakfast, I think, Joshua.

CLIVE and JOSHUA go in. HARRY is following.

EDWARD. Uncle.

HARRY stops.

EDWARD. Harry, why won't you talk to me?

HARRY. Of course I'll talk to you.

EDWARD. If you won't be nice to me I'll tell father.

HARRY. Edward, no, not a word, never, not to your mother, nobody, please. Edward, do you understand? Please.

EDWARD. I won't tell. I promise I'll never tell. I've cut my finger and sworn.

HARRY.	There's no need to get so excited Edward. We can't be together all the time. I will have to leave soon anyway, and go back to the river.
EDWARD.	You can't, you can't go. Take me with you.
ELLEN.	Edward!
HARRY.	I have my duty to the Empire.

HARRY goes in. ELLEN comes out.

ELLEN.	Edward, breakfast time. Edward.
EDWARD.	I'm not hungry.
ELLEN.	Betty, please come and speak to Edward.

BETTY comes.

BETTY.	Why, what's the matter?
ELLEN.	He won't come in for breakfast.
BETTY.	Edward, I shall call your father.
EDWARD.	You can't make me eat.

He goes in. BETTY is about to follow.

ELLEN.	Betty.

BETTY stops.

ELLEN.	Betty, when Edward goes to school will I have to leave?
BETTY.	Never mind, Ellen dear, you'll get another place. I'll give you an excellent reference.
ELLEN.	I don't want another place, Betty. I want to stay with you forever.
BETTY.	If you go back to England you might get married, Ellen. You're quite pretty, you shouldn't despair of getting a husband.
ELLEN.	I don't want a husband. I want you.
BETTY.	Children of your own, Ellen, think.
ELLEN.	I don't want children, I don't like children. I just want to be alone with you, Betty, and sing for you and kiss you because I love you, Betty.

BETTY. I love you too, Ellen. But women have their duty as soldiers have. You must be a mother if you can.

ELLEN. Betty, Betty, I love you so much. I want to stay with you forever, my love for you is eternal, stronger than death. I'd rather die than leave you, Betty.

BETTY. No you wouldn't, Ellen, don't be silly. Come, don't cry. You don't feel what you think you do. It's the loneliness here and the climate is very confusing. Come and have breakfast, Ellen dear, and I'll forget all about it.

ELLEN goes. CLIVE comes.

BETTY. Clive, please forgive me.

CLIVE. Will you leave me alone?

BETTY goes back into the house. HARRY comes.

CLIVE. Women, Harry. I envy you going into the jungle, a man's life.

HARRY. I envy you.

CLIVE. Harry, I know you do. I have spoken to Betty.

HARRY. I assure you, Clive —

CLIVE. Please say nothing about it.

HARRY. My friendship for you —

CLIVE. Absolutely. I know the friendship between us, Harry, is not something that could be spoiled by the weaker sex. Friendship between men is a fine thing. It is the noblest form of relationship.

HARRY. I agree with you.

CLIVE. There is the necessity of reproduction. The family is all important. And there is the pleasure. But what we put ourselves through to get the pleasure, Harry. When I heard about our fine fellows last night fighting those savages to protect us I thought yes, that is what I aspire to. I tell you Harry, in confidence, I suddenly got out of Mrs Saunders' bed and came out here on the verandah and looked at the stars.

HARRY.   I couldn't sleep last night either.

CLIVE.   There is something dark about women, that threatens what is best in us. Between men that light burns brightly.

HARRY.   I didn't know you felt like that.

CLIVE.   Women are irrational, demanding, inconsistent, treacherous, lustful, and they smell different from us.

HARRY.   Clive —

CLIVE.   Think of the comradeship of men, Harry, sharing adventures, sharing danger, risking their lives together.

HARRY *takes hold of* CLIVE.

CLIVE.   What are you doing?

HARRY.   Well, you said —

CLIVE.   I said what?

HARRY.   Between men.

CLIVE *is speechless*.

I'm sorry, I misunderstood, I would never have dreamt, I thought —

CLIVE.   My God, Harry, how disgusting.

HARRY.   You will not betray my confidence.

CLIVE.   I feel contaminated.

HARRY.   I struggle against it. You cannot imagine the shame. I have tried everything to save myself.

CLIVE.   The most revolting perversion. Rome fell, Harry, and this sin can destroy an empire.

HARRY.   It is not a sin, it is a disease.

CLIVE.   A disease more dangerous than diphtheria. Effeminacy is contagious. How I have been deceived. Your face does not look degenerate. Oh Harry, how did you sink to this?

HARRY.   Clive, help me, what am I to do?

CLIVE.   You have been away from England too long.

HARRY.   Where can I go except into the jungle to hide?

CLIVE.   You don't do it with the natives, Harry? My God, what a betrayal of the Queen.

HARRY.   Clive, I am like a man born crippled. Please help me.

CLIVE.   You must repent.

HARRY.   I have thought of killing myself.

CLIVE.   That is a sin too.

HARRY.   There is no way out. Clive, I beg of you, do not betray my confidence.

CLIVE.   I cannot keep a secret like this. Rivers will be named after you, it's unthinkable. You must save yourself from depravity. You must get married. You are not unattractive to women. What a relief that you and Betty were not after all — good God, how disgusting. Now Mrs Saunders. She's a woman of spirit, she could go with you on your expeditions.

HARRY.   I suppose getting married wouldn't be any worse than killing myself.

CLIVE.   Mrs Saunders! Mrs Saunders! Ask her now, Harry. Think of England.

MRS SAUNDERS *comes*. CLIVE *withdraws*. HARRY *goes up to* MRS SAUNDERS.

HARRY.   Mrs Saunders, will you marry me?

MRS SAUNDERS.   Why?

HARRY.   We are both alone.

MRS SAUNDERS.   I choose to be alone, Mr Bagley. If I can look after myself, I'm sure you can. Clive, I have something important to tell you. I've just found Joshua putting earth on his head. He tells me his parents were killed last night by the British soldiers. I think you owe him an apology on behalf of the Queen.

CLIVE.   Joshua! Joshua!

MRS SAUNDERS.   Mr Bagley, I could never be a wife again.
                There is only one thing about marriage that I
                like.

                JOSHUA *comes*.

CLIVE.   Joshua, I am horrified to hear what has
                happened. Good God!

MRS SAUNDERS.   His father was shot. His mother died in
                the blaze.

                MRS SAUNDERS *goes*.

CLIVE.   Joshua, do you want a day off? Do you want to
                go to your people?

JOSHUA.   Not my people, sir.

CLIVE.   But you want to go to your parents' funeral?

JOSHUA.   No sir.

CLIVE.   Yes, Joshua, yes, your father and mother. I'm
                sure they were loyal to the crown. I'm sure it was
                all a terrible mistake.

JOSHUA.   My mother and father were bad people.

CLIVE.   Joshua, no.

JOSHUA.   You are my father and mother.

CLIVE.   Well really. I don't know what to say. That's very
                decent of you. Are you sure there's nothing I can
                do? You can have the day off you know.

                BETTY *comes out followed by* EDWARD.

BETTY.   What's the matter? What's happening?

CLIVE.   Something terrible has happened. No, I mean
                some relatives of Joshua's met with an accident.

JOSHUA.   May I go sir?

CLIVE.   Yes, yes of course. Good God, what a terrible
                thing. Bring us a drink will you Joshua?

                JOSHUA *goes*.

EDWARD.   What? What?

BETTY.	Edward, go and do your lessons.
EDWARD.	What is it, Uncle Harry?
HARRY.	Go and do your lessons.
ELLEN.	Edward, come in here at once.
EDWARD.	What's happened, Uncle Harry?
	HARRY *has moved aside.* EDWARD *follows him.* ELLEN *comes out.*
HARRY.	Go away. Go inside. Ellen!
ELLEN.	Go inside, Edward. I shall tell your mother.
BETTY.	Go inside, Edward at once. I shall tell your father.
CLIVE.	Go inside, Edward. And Betty you go inside too.
	BETTY, EDWARD *and* ELLEN *go.* MAUD *comes out.*
CLIVE.	Go inside. And Ellen, you come outside.
	ELLEN *comes out.*
	Mr Bagley has something to say to you.
HARRY.	Ellen. I don't suppose you would marry me?
ELLEN.	What if I said yes?
CLIVE.	Run along now, you two want to be alone.
	HARRY *and* ELLEN *go out.* JOSHUA *brings* CLIVE *a drink.*
JOSHUA.	The governess and your wife, sir.
CLIVE.	What's that, Joshua?
JOSHUA.	She talks of love to your wife, sir. I have seen them. Bad women.
CLIVE.	Joshua, you go too far. Get out of my sight.

Scene Five

The verandah. A table with a white cloth. A wedding cake and a large knife. Bottles and glasses. JOSHUA *is putting things on the table.* EDWARD *has the doll.* JOSHUA *sees him with it. He holds out his hand.* EDWARD *gives him the doll.* JOSHUA *takes the knife and cuts the doll open and shakes the sawdust out of it.* JOSHUA *throws the doll under the table.*

MAUD. Come along Edward, this is such fun.

    Everyone enters, triumphal arch for HARRY *and* ELLEN.

    Your mama's wedding was a splendid occasion, Edward. I cried and cried.

    ELLEN *and* BETTY *go aside.*

ELLEN. Betty, what happens with a man? I don't know what to do.

BETTY. You just keep still.

ELLEN. And what does he do?

BETTY. Harry will know what to do.

ELLEN. And is it enjoyable?

BETTY. Ellen, you're not getting married to enjoy yourself.

ELLEN. Don't forget me, Betty.

    ELLEN *goes.*

BETTY. I think my necklace has been stolen Clive. I did so want to wear it at the wedding.

EDWARD. It was Joshua. Joshua took it.

CLIVE. Joshua?

EDWARD. He did, he did, I saw him with it.

HARRY. Edward, that's not true.

EDWARD. It is, it is.

HARRY. Edward, I'm afraid you took it yourself.

EDWARD. I did not.

HARRY.   I have seen him with it.

CLIVE.   Edward, is that true? Where is it? Did you take
           your mother's necklace? And to try and blame
           Joshua, good God.

           EDWARD *runs off.*

BETTY.   Edward, come back. Have you got my necklace?

HARRY.   I should leave him alone. He'll bring it back.

BETTY.   I wanted to wear it. I wanted to look my best at
           your wedding.

HARRY.   You always look your best to me.

BETTY.   I shall get drunk.

           MRS SAUNDERS *comes.*

MRS SAUNDERS.   The sale of my property is completed. I
           shall leave tomorrow.

CLIVE.   That's just as well. Whose protection will you
           seek this time?

MRS SAUNDERS.   I shall go to England and buy a farm
           there. I shall introduce threshing machines.

CLIVE.   Amazing spirit.

           He *kisses her.* BETTY *launches herself on* MRS
           SAUNDERS. *They fall to the ground.*

CLIVE.   Betty — Caroline — I don't deserve this —
           Harry, Harry.

           HARRY *and* CLIVE *separate them.* HARRY *holding*
           MRS SAUNDERS, CLIVE BETTY.

CLIVE.   Mrs Saunders, how can you abuse my
           hospitality? How dare you touch my wife? You
           must leave here at once.

BETTY.   Go away, go away. You are a wicked woman.

MAUD.   Mrs Saunders, I am shocked. This is your
           hostess.

CLIVE.   Pack your bags and leave the house this instant.

MRS SAUNDERS.   I was leaving anyway. There's no place

for me here. I have made arrangements to leave tomorrow, and tomorrow is when I will leave. I wish you joy, Mr Bagley.

MRS SAUNDERS *goes*.

CLIVE.   No place for her anywhere I should think. Shocking behaviour.

BETTY.   Oh Clive, forgive me, and love me like you used to.

CLIVE.   Were you jealous my dove? My own dear wife!

MAUD.   Ah, Mr Bagley, one flesh, you see.

EDWARD *comes back with the necklace*.

CLIVE.   Good God, Edward, it's true.

EDWARD.   I was minding it for mama because of the troubles.

CLIVE.   Well done, Edward, that was very manly of you. See Betty? Edward was protecting his mama's jewels from the rebels. What a hysterical fuss over nothing. Well done, little man. It is quite safe now. The bad men are dead. Edward, you may do up the necklace for mama.

EDWARD *does up* BETTY's *necklace, supervised by* CLIVE. JOSHUA *is drinking steadily*. ELLEN *comes back*.

MAUD.   Ah, here's the bride. Come along, Ellen, you don't cry at your own wedding, only at other people's.

CLIVE.   Now, speeches, speeches. Who is going to make a speech? Harry, make a speech.

HARRY.   I'm no speaker. You're the one for that.

ALL.   Speech, speech.

HARRY.   My dear friends — what can I say — the empire — the family — the married state to which I have always aspired — your shining example of domestic bliss — my great good fortune in winning Ellen's love — happiest day of my life.

Applause.

CLIVE.   Cut the cake, cut the cake.

                HARRY and ELLEN take the knife to cut the cake.
                HARRY steps on the doll under the table.

HARRY.   What's this?

ELLEN.   Oh look.

BETTY.   Edward.

EDWARD.   It was Joshua. It was Joshua. I saw him.

CLIVE.   Don't tell lies again.

                He hits EDWARD across the side of the head.

                Unaccustomed as I am to public speaking —

                Cheers.

                Harry, my friend. So brave and strong and
                supple. Ellen, from neath her veil so shyly
                peeking. I wish you joy. A toast — the happy
                couple. Dangers are past. Our enemies are
                killed. — Put your arm around her, Harry, have
                a kiss — All murmuring of discontent is stilled.
                Long may you live in peace and joy and bliss.

                While he is speaking JOSHUA raises his gun to
                shoot CLIVE. Only EDWARD sees. He does nothing
                to warn the others. He put his hands over his ears.
                BLACK.

ACT TWO

Scene One

Winter afternoon. Inside the hut of a one o'clock club, a children's playcentre in a park, VICTORIA and LIN, mothers. CATHY, LIN's daughter, aged 4, played by a man, clinging to LIN. VICTORIA reading a book.

CATHY.   Yum yum bubblegum.
          Stick it up your mother's bum.
          When it's brown
          Pull it down
          Yum yum bubblegum.

LIN.   Like your shoes, Victoria.

CATHY.   Jack be nimble, Jack be quick,
          Jack jump over the candlestick.
          Silly Jack, he should jump higher,
          Goodness gracious, great balls of fire.

LIN.   Cathy, do stop. Do a painting.

CATHY.   You do a painting.

LIN.   You do a painting.

CATHY.   What shall I paint?

LIN.   Paint a house.

CATHY.   No.

LIN.   Princess.

CATHY.   No.

LIN.   Pirates.

CATHY.   Already done that.

LIN.   Spacemen.

CATHY.   I never paint spacemen. You know I never.

LIN.   Paint a car crash and blood everywhere.

CATHY.   No, don't tell me. I know what to paint.

LIN.   Go on then. You need an apron, where's an apron. Here.

CATHY.   Don't want an apron.

LIN.   Lift up your arms. There's a good girl.

CATHY.   I don't want to paint.

LIN.   Don't paint. Don't paint.

CATHY.   What shall I do? You paint. What shall I do mum?

VICTORIA. There's nobody on the big bike, Cathy, quick.

           CATHY goes out. VICTORIA is watching the children playing outside.

VICTORIA. Tommy, it's Jimmy's gun. Let him have it. What the hell.

           She goes on reading. She reads while she talks.

LIN.   I don't know how you can concentrate.

VICTORIA. You have to or you never do anything.

LIN.   Yeh, well. It's really warm in here, that's one thing. It's better than standing out there. I got chilblains last winter.

VICTORIA. It is warm.

LIN.   I suppose Tommy doesn't let you read much. I expect he talks to you while you're reading.

VICTORIA. Yes, he does.

LIN.   I didn't get very far with that book you lent me.

VICTORIA. That's all right.

LIN.   I was glad to have it, though. I sit with it on my lap while I'm watching telly. Well, Cathy's off. She's frightened I'm going to leave her. It's the babyminder didn't work out when she

was two, she still remembers. You can't get
them used to other people if you're by
yourself. It's no good blaming me. She clings
round my knees every morning up the nursery
and they don't say anything but they make
you feel you're making her do it. But I'm
desperate for her to go to school. I did cry
when I left her the first day. You wouldn't,
you're too fucking sensible. You'll call the
teacher by her first name. I really fancy you.

VICTORIA. What?

LIN.   Put your book down will you for five minutes.
             You didn't hear a word I said.

VICTORIA. I don't get much time to myself.

LIN.   Do you ever go to the movies?

VICTORIA. Tommy's very funny who he's left with. My
             mother babysits sometimes.

LIN.   Your husband could babysit.

VICTORIA. But then we couldn't go to the movies.

LIN.   You could go to the movies with me.

VICTORIA. Oh I see.

LIN.   Couldn't you?

VICTORIA. Well yes, I could.

LIN.   Friday night?

VICTORIA. What film are we talking about?

LIN.   Does it matter what film?

VICTORIA. Of course it does.

LIN.   You choose then. Friday night.

             CATHY *comes in with gun, shoots them saying kiou
             kiou kiou, and runs off again.*

             Not in a foreign language, OK. You don't go
             to the movies to read.

             LIN *watches the children playing outside.*

Don't hit him, Cathy, kill him. Point the gun,
kiou, kiou, kiou. That's the way.

VICTORIA. They've just banned war toys in Sweden.

LIN. The kids'll just hit each other more.

VICTORIA. Well, psychologists do differ in their opinions
as to whether or not aggression is innate.

LIN. Yeh?

VICTORIA. I'm afraid I do let Tommy play with guns and
just hope he'll get it out of his system and not
end up in the army.

LIN. I've got a brother in the army.

VICTORIA. Oh I'm sorry. Whereabouts is he stationed?

LIN. Belfast.

VICTORIA. Oh dear.

LIN. I've got a friend who's Irish and we went on a
Troops Out march. Now my dad won't speak
to me.

VICTORIA. I don't get on too well with my father either.

LIN. And your husband? How do you get on with
him?

VICTORIA. Oh, fine. Up and down. You know. Very well.
He helps with the washing up and everything.

LIN. I left mine two years ago. He let me keep
Cathy and I'm grateful for that.

VICTORIA. You shouldn't be grateful.

LIN. I'm a lesbian.

VICTORIA. You still shouldn't be grateful.

LIN. I'm grateful he didn't hit me harder than he
did.

VICTORIA. I suppose I'm very lucky with Martin.

LIN. Don't get at me about how I bring up Cathy,
OK?

VICTORIA. I didn't.

LIN.   Yes you did. War toys. I'll give her a rifle for
             Christmas and blast Tommy's pretty head off
             for a start.

             VICTORIA *goes back to her book.*

LIN.   I hate men.

VICTORIA.   You have to look at it in a historical
             perspective in terms of learnt behaviour since
             the industrial revolution.

LIN.   I just hate the bastards.

VICTORIA.   Well it's a point of view.

             By now CATHY *has come back in and started
             painting in many colours, without an apron.*
             EDWARD *comes in.*

EDWARD.   Victoria, mother's in the park. She's walking
             round all the paths very fast.

VICTORIA.   By herself?

EDWARD.   I told her you were here.

VICTORIA.   Thanks.

EDWARD.   Come on.

VICTORIA.   Ten minutes talking to my mother and I have
             to spend two hours in a hot bath.

             VICTORIA *goes out.*

LIN.   Shit, Cathy, what about an apron. I don't
             mind you having paint on your frock but if it
             doesn't wash off just don't tell me you can't
             wear a frock with paint on, OK?

CATHY.   OK.

LIN.   You're gay, aren't you?

EDWARD.   I beg your pardon?

LIN.   I really fancy your sister. I thought you'd
             understand. You do but you can go on
             pretending you don't, I don't mind. That's
             lovely Cathy, I like the green bit.

EDWARD. Don't go around saying that. I might lose my job.

LIN. The last gardener was ever so straight. He used to flash at all the little girls.

EDWARD. I wish you hadn't said that about me. It's not true.

LIN. It's not true and I never said it and I never thought it and I never will think it again.

EDWARD. Someone might have heard you.

LIN. Shut up about it then.

BETTY *and* VICTORIA *come up.*

BETTY. It's quite a nasty bump.

VICTORIA. He's not even crying.

BETTY. I think that's very worrying. You and Edward always cried. Perhaps he's got concussion.

VICTORIA. Of course he hasn't mummy.

BETTY. That other little boy was very rough. Should you speak to somebody about him?

VICTORIA. Tommy was hitting him with a spade.

BETTY. Well he's a real little boy. And so brave not to cry. You must watch him for signs of drowsiness. And nausea. If he's sick in the night, phone an ambulance. Well, you're looking very well darling, a bit tired, a bit peaky. I think the fresh air agrees with Edward. He likes the open air life because of growing up in Africa. He misses the sunshine, don't you, darling? We'll soon have Edward back on his feet. What fun it is here.

VICTORIA. This is Lin. And Cathy.

BETTY. Oh Cathy what a lovely painting. What is it? Well I think it's a house on fire. I think all that red is a fire. Is that right? Or do I see legs, is it a horse? Can I have the lovely painting or is it for mummy? Children have such imagination, it makes them so exhausting. (*To* LIN.) I'm sure you're wonderful, just like Victoria. I had help with my children. One does need help. That was in Africa of course so there wasn't the servant problem. This is my son Edward. This is —

EDWARD.   Lin.

BETTY.   Lin, this is Lin. Edward is doing something such fun, he's working in the park as a gardener. He does look exactly like a gardener.

EDWARD.   I am a gardener.

BETTY.   He's certainly making a stab at it. Well it will be a story to tell. I expect he will write a novel about it, or perhaps a television series. Well what a pretty child Cathy is. Victoria was a pretty child just like a little doll – you can't be certain how they'll grow up. I think Victoria's very pretty but she doesn't make the most of herself, do you darling, it's not the fashion I'm told but there are still women who dress out of *Vogue*, well we hope that's not what Martin looks for, though in many ways I wish it was, I don't know what it is Martin looks for and nor does he I'm afraid poor Martin. Well I am rattling on. I like your skirt dear but your shoes won't do at all. Well do they have lady gardeners, Edward, because I'm going to leave your father and I think I might need to get a job, not a gardener really of course. I haven't got green fingers I'm afraid, everything I touch shrivels straight up. Vicky gave me a poinsettia last Christmas and the leaves all fell off on Boxing Day. Well good heavens, look what's happened to that lovely painting.

CATHY *has slowly and carefully been going over the whole sheet with black paint. She has almost finished.*

LIN.   What you do that for silly? It was nice.

CATHY.   I like your earrings.

VICTORIA. Did you say you're leaving Daddy?

BETTY.   Do you darling? Shall I put them on you? My ears aren't pierced, I never wanted that, they just clip on the lobe.

LIN.   She'll get paint on you, mind.

BETTY.   There's a pretty girl. It doesn't hurt does it? Well you'll grow up to know you have to suffer a little bit for beauty.

CATHY.   Look mum I'm pretty, I'm pretty, I'm pretty.

LIN.   Stop showing off Cathy.

VICTORIA. It's time we went home. Tommy, time to go home. Last go then, all right.

EDWARD.   Mum did I hear you right just now?

CATHY.   I want my ears pierced.

BETTY.   Ooh, not till you're big.

CATHY.   I know a girl got her ears pierced and she's three. She's got real gold.

BETTY.   I don't expect she's English, darling. Can I give her a sweety? I know they're not very good for the teeth, Vicky gets terribly cross with me. What does mummy say?

LIN.   Just one, thank you very much.

CATHY.   I like your beads.

BETTY.   Yes they are pretty. Here you are.

It is the necklace from Act One.

CATHY.   Look at me, look at me. Vicky, Vicky look at me.

LIN.   You look lovely, come on now.

CATHY.   And your hat, and your hat.

LIN.   No, that's enough.

BETTY.   Of course she can have my hat.

CATHY.   Yes, yes, hat, hat. Look look look.

LIN.   That's enough, please, stop it now. Hat off, bye
            bye hat.

CATHY.   Give me my hat.

LIN.   Bye bye beads.

BETTY.   It's just fun.

LIN.   It's very nice of you.

CATHY.   I want my beads.

LIN.   Where's the other earring?

CATHY.   I want my beads.

            CATHY *has the other earring in her hand.*
            Meanwhile VICTORIA *and* EDWARD *look for it.*

EDWARD.   Is it on the floor?

VICTORIA.   Don't step on it.

EDWARD.   Where?

CATHY.   I want my beads. I want my beads.

LIN.   You'll have a smack.

            LIN *gets the earring from* CATHY.

CATHY.   I want my beads.

BETTY.   Oh dear oh dear. Have you got the earring?
            Thank you darling.

CATHY.   I want my beads, you're horrid, I hate you,
            mum, you smell.

BETTY.   This is the point you see where one had help.
            Well it's been lovely seeing you dears and I'll
            be off again on my little walk.

VICTORIA.   You're leaving him? Really?

BETTY.   Yes your hear aright, Vicky, yes. I'm finding a
            little flat, that will be fun. Bye bye Tommy,
            granny's going now. Tommy don't hit that
            little girl, say goodbye to granny.

            BETTY *goes.*

VICTORIA.   Fucking hell.

EDWARD. Puking Jesus.

LIN. That was news was it, leaving your father?

EDWARD. They're going to want so much attention.

VICTORIA. Does everybody hate their mothers?

EDWARD. Mind you, I wouldn't live with him.

LIN. Stop snivelling, pigface. Where's your coat? Be quiet now and we'll have doughnuts for tea and if you keep on we'll have dogshit on toast.

CATHY laughs so much she lies on the floor.

VICTORIA. Tommy, you've have two last goes. Last last last last go.

LIN. Not that funny, come on, coat on.

EDWARD. Can I have your painting?

CATHY. What for?

EDWARD. For a friend of mine.

CATHY. What's his name?

EDWARD. Gerry.

CATHY. How old is he?

EDWARD. Thirty-two.

CATHY. You can if you like. I don't care. Kiou kiou kiou kiou.

CATHY goes out. EDWARD takes the painting and goes out.

LIN. Will you have sex with me?

VICTORIA. I don't know what Martin would say. Does it count as adultery with a woman?

LIN. You'd enjoy it.

Scene Two

Spring. Swing, bench, pond nearby. EDWARD *is gardening.*
GERRY *is sitting on a bench.*

EDWARD. I sometimes pretend we don't know each
other. And you've come to the park to eat
your sandwiches and look at me.

GERRY. That would be more interesting, yes. Come
and sit down.

EDWARD. If the superintendent comes I'll be in trouble.
It's not my dinner time yet. Where were you
last night? I think you owe me an explanation.
We always do tell each other everything.

GERRY. Is that a rule?

EDWARD. It's what we agreed.

GERRY. It's a habit we've got into. Look, I was drunk.
I woke up at 4 o'clock on somebody's floor. I
was sick. I hadn't any money for a cab. I went
back to sleep.

EDWARD. You could have phoned.

GERRY. There wasn't a phone.

EDWARD. Sorry.

GERRY. There was a phone and I didn't phone you.
Leave it alone, Eddy, I'm warning you.

EDWARD. What are you going to do to me, then?

GERRY. I'm going to the pub.

EDWARD. I'll join you in ten minutes.

GERRY. I didn't ask you to come.

EDWARD *goes.*

Two years I've been with Edward. You have to
get away sometimes or you lose sight of
yourself. The train from Victoria to Clapham
still has those compartments without a
corridor. As soon as I got on the platform I
saw who I wanted. Slim hips, tense shoulders,

trying not to look at anyone. I put my hand
on my packet just long enough so that he
couldn't miss it. The train came in. You don't
want to get in too fast or some straight dumbo
might get in with you. I sat by the window. I
couldn't see where the fuck he'd got to. Then
just as the whistle went he got in. Great. It's a
six minute journey so you can't start anything
you can't finish. I stared at him and he
unzipped his flies. Then he stopped. So I
stood up and took my cock out. He took me
in his mouth and shut his eyes tight. He was
sort of mumbling it about as if he wasn't sure
what to do, so I said, 'A bit tighter son' and
he said 'Sorry' and then got on with it. He was
jerking off with his left hand, and I could see
he'd got a fairsized one. I wished he'd keep
still so I could see his watch. I was getting
really turned on. What if we pulled into
Clapham Junction now. Of course by the time
we sat down again the train was just slowing
up. I felt wonderful. Then he started talking.
It's better if nothing is said. Once you find
he's a librarian in Walthamstow with a special
interest in science fiction and lives with his
aunt, then forget it. He said I hope you don't
think I do this all the time. I said I hope you
will from now on. He said he would if I was
on the train, but why don't we go out for a
meal? I opened the door before the train
stopped. I told him I lived with somebody. I
don't want to know. He was jogging sideways
to keep up. He said 'What's your phone
number, you're my ideal physical type, what
sign of the zodiac are you? Where do you
live? Where are you going now? It's not fair.' I
saw him at Victoria a couple of months later
and I went straight down to the end of the
platform and I picked up somebody really
great who never said a word, just smiled.

CATHY *is on the swing.*

CATHY.   Batman and Robin

Had a batmobile.
Robin done a fart
And paralysed the wheel.
The wheel couldn't take it,
The engine fell apart,
All because of Robin
And his supersonic fart.

CATHY *goes*. MARTIN, VICTORIA *and*
BETTY *walking slowly*.

MARTIN.   Tom!

BETTY.   He'll fall in.

VICTORIA.   No he won't.

MARTIN.   Don't go too near the edge, Tom. Throw the
            bread from there. The ducks can get it.

BETTY.   I'll never be able to manage. If I can't even
            walk down the street by myself. Everything
            looks so fierce.

VICTORIA.   Just watch Tommy feeding the ducks.

BETTY.   He's going to fall in. Make Martin make him
            move back.

VICTORIA.   He's not going to fall in.

BETTY.   It's since I left your father.

VICTORIA.   Mummy, it really was the right decision.

BETTY.   Everything comes at me from all directions.
            Martin despises me.

VICTORIA.   Of course he doesn't mummy.

BETTY.   Of course he does.

MARTIN.   Throw the bread. That's the way. The duck
            can get it. Quack quack quack quack quack.

BETTY.   I don't want to take pills. Lin says you can't
            trust doctors.

VICTORIA.   You're not taking pills. You're doing very well.

BETTY.   But I'm so frightened.

VICTORIA.   What are you frightened of?

BETTY.   Victoria, you always ask that as if there was suddenly going to be an answer.

VICTORIA.   Are you all right sitting there?

BETTY.   Yes, yes. Go and be with Martin.

VICTORIA joins MARTIN. BETTY stays sitting on the bench.

MARTIN.   You take the job, you go to Manchester. You turn it down, you stay in London. People are making decisions like this every day of the week. It needn't be for more than a year. You get long vacations. Our relationship might well stand the strain of that, and if it doesn't we're better out of it. I don't want to put any pressure on you. I'd just like to know so we can sell the house. I think we're moving into an entirely different way of life if you go to Manchester because it won't end there. We could keep the house as security for Tommy but he might as well get used to the fact that life nowadays is insecure. You should ask your mother what she thinks and then do the opposite. I could just take that room in Barbara's house, and then we could babysit for each other. You think that means I want to fuck Barbara. I don't. Well I do, but I won't. And even if I did, what's a fuck between friends? Who are we meant to do it with, strangers? Whatever you want to do, I'll be delighted. If you could just let me know what it is I'm to be delighted about. Don't cry again, Vicky, I'm not the sort of man who makes women cry.

LIN has come in and sat down with BETTY. CATHY joins them. She is wearing a pink dress and carrying a rifle.

LIN.   I've bought her three new frocks. She won't wear jeans to school any more because Tracy and Mandy called her a boy.

CATHY.   Tracy's got a perm.

LIN.	You should have shot them.
CATHY.	They're coming to tea and we've got to have trifle. Not trifle you make, trifle out of a packet. And you've got to wear a skirt. And tights.
LIN.	Tracy's mum wears jeans.
CATHY.	She does not. She wears velvet.
BETTY.	Well I think you look very pretty. And if that gun has caps in it please take it a long way away.
CATHY.	It's got red caps. They're louder.
MARTIN.	Do you think you're well enough to do this job? You don't have to do it. No one's going to think any the less of you if you stay here with me. There's no point being so liberated you make yourself cry all the time. You stay and we'll get everything sorted out. What it is about sex, when we talk while it's happening I get to feel it's like a driving lesson. Left, right, a little faster, carry on, slow down—

CATHY *shoots* VICTORIA.

CATHY.	You're dead Vicky.
VICTORIA.	Aaaargh.
CATHY.	Fall over.
VICTORIA.	I'm not falling over, the ground's wet.
CATHY.	You're dead.
VICTORIA.	Yes, I'm dead.
CATHY.	The Dead Hand Gang fall over. They said I had to fall over in the mud or I can't play. That duck's a mandarin.
MARTIN.	Which one? Look, Tommy?
CATHY.	That's a diver. It's got a yellow eye and it dives. That's a goose. Tommy doesn't know it's a goose, he thinks it's a duck. The babies get eaten by weasels. Kiou kiou.

CATHY *goes.*

MARTIN. So I lost my erection last night, not because I'm not prepared to talk, it's just that taking in technical information is a different part of the brain and also I don't like to feel that you do it better to yourself. I have read the Hite report. I do know that women have to learn to get their pleasure despite our clumsy attempts at expressing undying devotion and ecstasy, and that what we spent our adolescence thinking was an animal urge we had to suppress is in fact a fine art we have to acquire. I'm not like whatever percentage of American men have become impotent as a direct result of women's liberation, which I am totally in favour of, more I sometimes think than you are yourself. Nor am I one of your villains who sticks it in, bangs away, and falls asleep. My one aim is to give you pleasure. My one aim is to give you rolling orgasms like I do other women. So why the hell don't you have them? My analysis for what it's worth is that despite all my efforts you still feel dominated by me. I in fact think it's very sad that you don't feel able to take that job. It makes me feel very guilty. I don't want you to do it just because I encourage you to do it. But don't you think you'd feel better if you did take the job? You're the one who's talked about freedom. You're the one who's experimenting with bi-sexuality, and I don't stop you, I think women have something to give each other. You seem to need the mutual support. You find me too overwhelming. So follow it through, go away, leave me and Tommy alone for a bit, we can manage perfectly well without you. I'm not putting any pressure on you but I don't think you're being a whole person. God knows I do everything I can to make you stand on your own two feet. Just be yourself. You don't seem to realise how insulting it is to me that you can't get yourself together.

MARTIN *and* VICTORIA *go.*

BETTY.   You must be very lonely yourself with no
          husband. You don't miss him?

LIN.   Not really, no.

BETTY.   Maybe you like being on your own.

LIN.   I'm seeing quite a lot of Vicky. I don't live
          alone. I live with Cathy.

BETTY.   I would have been frightened when I was your
          age. I thought, the poor children, their mother
          all alone.

LIN.   I've a lot of friends.

BETTY.   I find when I'm making tea I put out two
          cups. It's strange not having a man in the
          house. You don't know who to do things for.

LIN.   Yourself.

BETTY.   Oh, that's very selfish.

LIN.   Have you any women friends?

BETTY.   I've never been so short of men's company
          that I've had to bother with women.

LIN.   Don't you like women?

BETTY.   They don't have such interesting conversations
          as men. There has never been a woman
          composer of genius. They don't have a sense
          of humour. They spoil things for themselves
          with their emotions. I can't say I do like
          women very much, no.

LIN.   But you're a woman.

BETTY.   There's nothing says you have to like yourself.

LIN.   Do you like me?

BETTY.   There's no need to take it personally, Lin.

MARTIN *and* VICTORIA *come back.*

MARTIN.   Do you know if you put cocaine on your prick
          you can keep up it all night? The only thing
          is of course it goes numb so you don't feel

anything. But you would, that's the main thing. I just want to make you happy.

BETTY. Vicky, I'd like to go home.

VICTORIA. Yes, mummy, of course.

BETTY. I'm sorry, dear.

VICTORIA. I think Tommy would like to stay out a bit longer.

LIN. Hello, Martin. We do keep out of each other's way.

MARTIN. I think that's the best thing to do.

BETTY. Perhaps you'd walk home with me, Martin. I do feel safer with a man. The park is so large the grass seems to tilt.

MARTIN. Yes, I'd like to go home and do some work. I'm writing a novel about women from the women's point of view.

MARTIN and BETTY go. LIN and VICTORIA are alone. They embrace.

VICTORIA. Why the hell can't he just be a wife and come with me? Why does Martin make me tie myself in knots? No wonder we can't just have a simple fuck. No, not Martin, why do I make myself tie myself in knots. It's got to stop, Lin. I'm not like that with you. Would you love me if I went to Manchester?

LIN. Yes.

VICTORIA. Would you love me if I went on a climbing expedition in the Andes mountains?

LIN. Yes.

VICTORIA. Would you love me if my teeth fell out?

LIN. Yes.

VICTORIA. Would you love me if I loved ten other people?

LIN. And me?

VICTORIA. Yes.

LIN.   Yes.

VICTORIA. And I feel apologetic for not being quite so
          subordinate as I was. I am more intelligent
          than him. I am brilliant.

LIN.   Leave him Vic. Come and live with me.

VICTORIA. Don't be silly.

LIN.   Silly, Christ, don't then. I'm not asking
          because I need to live with someone. I'd enjoy
          it, that's all, we'd both enjoy it. Fuck you.
          Cathy, for fuck's sake. stop throwing stones at
          the ducks. The man's going to get you.

VICTORIA. What man? Do you need a man to frighten
          your child with?

LIN.   My mother said it.

VICTORIA. You're so inconsistent, Lin.

LIN.   I've changed who I sleep with, I can't change
          everything.

VICTORIA. Like when I had to stop you getting a job in a
          boutique and collaborating with sexist
          consumerism.

LIN.   I should have got that job, Cathy would have
          liked it. Why shouldn't I have some decent
          clothes? I'm sick of dressing like a boy, why
          can't I look sexy, wouldn't you love me?

VICTORIA. Lin, you've no analysis.

LIN.   No but I'm good at kissing aren't I? I give
          Cathy guns, my mum didn't give me guns. I
          dress her in jeans, she wants to wear dresses. I
          don't know. I can't work it out, I don't want
          to. You read too many books, you get at me
          all the time, you're worse to me than Martin is
          to you, you piss me off, my brother's been
          killed. I'm sorry to win the argument that way
          but there it is.

VICTORIA. What do you mean win the argument?

LIN.   I mean be nice to me.

VICTORIA. In Belfast?

LIN.   I heard this morning. Don't don't start. I've hardly seen him for two years. I rung my father. You'd think I shot him myself. He doesn't want me to go to the funeral.

CATHY approaches.

VICTORIA. What will you do?

LIN.   Go of course.

CATHY.   What it is? Who's killed? What?

LIN.   It's Bill. Your uncle. In the army. Bill that gave you the blue teddy.

CATHY.   Can I have his gun?

LIN.   It's time we went home. Time you went to bed.

CATHY.   No it's not.

LIN.   We go home and you have tea and you have a bath and you go to bed.

CATHY.   Fuck off.

LIN.   Cathy, shut up.

VICTORIA. It's only half past five, why don't we—

LIN.   I'll tell you why she has to go to bed—

VICTORIA. She can come home with me.

LIN.   Because I want her out the fucking way.

VICTORIA. She can come home with me.

CATHY.   I'm not going to bed.

LIN.   I want her home with me not home with you, I want her in bed, I want today over.

CATHY.   I'm not going to bed.

LIN hits CATHY, CATHY cries.

LIN.   And shut up or I'll give you something to cry for.

CATHY.   I'm not going to bed.

VICTORIA. Cathy—

LIN.   You keep out of it.

VICTORIA. Lin for God's sake.

           They are all shouting. CATHY *runs off.* LIN *and*
           VICTORIA *are silent. Then they laugh and embrace.*

LIN.   Where's Tommy?

VICTORIA. What? Didn't he go with Martin?

LIN.   Did he?

VICTORIA. God oh God.

LIN.   Cathy! Cathy!

VICTORIA. I haven't thought about him. How could I not
           think about him? Tommy!

LIN.   Cathy! Come on, quick, I want some help.

VICTORIA. Tommy! Tommy!

           CATHY *comes back.*

LIN.   Where's Tommy? Have you seen him? Did he
           go with Martin? Do you know where he is?

CATHY.   I showed him the goose. We went in the
           bushes.

LIN.   Then what?

CATHY.   I came back on the swing.

VICTORIA. And Tommy? Where was Tommy?

CATHY.   He fed the ducks.

LIN.   No that was before.

CATHY.   He did a pee in the bushes. I helped him with
           his trousers.

VICTORIA. And after that?

CATHY.   He fed the ducks.

VICTORIA. No no.

CATHY.   He liked the ducks. I expect he fell in.

LIN.   Did you see him fall in?

VICTORIA. Tommy! Tommy!

LIN.   What's the last time you saw him?

CATHY.   He did a pee.

VICTORIA. Mummy said he would fall in. Oh God,
               Tommy!

LIN.   We'll go round the pond. We'll go opposite
               ways round the pond.

ALL. *(Shout)*: Tommy!

               VICTORIA *and* LIN *go off opposite sides.* CATHY
               climbs the bench.

CATHY.   George Best, superstar
               Walks like a woman and wears a bra.
               There he is! I see him! Mum! Vicky! There he
               is! He's in the bushes.

               LIN *comes back.*

LIN.   Come on Cathy love, let's go home.

CATHY.   Vicky's got him.

LIN.   Come on.

CATHY.   Is she cross?

LIN.   No. Come on.

CATHY.   I found him.

LIN.   Yes. Come on.

               CATHY *gets off the bench.* CATHY *and* LIN *hug.*

CATHY.   I'm watching telly.

LIN.   OK.

CATHY.   After the news.

LIN.   OK.

CATHY.   I'm not going to bed.

LIN.   Yes you are.

CATHY.   I'm not going to bed now.

LIN.   Not now but early.

CATHY.   How early?

LIN.   Not late.

CATHY.   How not late?

LIN.   Early.

CATHY.   How early?

LIN.   Not late.

They go off together. GERRY *comes on. He waits.*
EDWARD *comes.*

EDWARD.   I've got some fish for dinner. I thought I'd
          make a cheese sauce.

GERRY.   I won't be in.

EDWARD.   Where are you going?

GERRY.   For a start I'm going to a sauna. Then I'll see.

EDWARD.   All right. What time will you be back? We'll
          eat then.

GERRY.   You're getting like a wife.

EDWARD.   I don't mind that.

GERRY.   Why don't I do the cooking sometime?

EDWARD.   You can if you like. You're just not as good at
          it that's all. Do it tonight.

GERRY.   I won't be in tonight.

EDWARD.   Do it tomorrow. If we can't eat it we can
          always go to a restaurant.

GERRY.   Stop it.

EDWARD.   Stop what?

GERRY.   Just be yourself.

EDWARD.   I don't know what you mean. Everyone's
          always tried to stop me being feminine and
          now you are too.

GERRY.   You're putting it on.

EDWARD.   I like doing the cooking. I like being fucked.
          You do like me like this really.

GERRY.   I'm bored, Eddy.

EDWARD.   Go to the sauna.

GERRY.   And you'll stay home and wait up for me.

EDWARD.   No, I'll go to bed and read a book.

GERRY.   Or knit. You could knit me a pair of socks.

EDWARD.   I might knit. I like knitting.

GERRY.   I don't mind if you knit. I don't want to be married.

EDWARD.   I do.

GERRY.   Well I'm divorcing you.

EDWARD.   I wouldn't want to keep a man who wants his freedom.

GERRY.   Eddy, do stop playing the injured wife, it's not funny.

EDWARD.   I'm not playing. It's true.

GERRY.   I'm not the husband so you can't be the wife.

EDWARD.   I'll always be here, Gerry, if you want to come back. I know you men like to go off by yourselves. I don't think I could love deeply more than once. But I don't think I can face life on my own so don't leave it too long or it may be too late.

GERRY.   What are you trying to turn me into?

EDWARD.   A monster, darling, which is what you are.

GERRY.   I'll collect my stuff from the flat in the morning.

            GERRY goes. EDWARD sits on the bench. It gets darker. VICTORIA comes.

VICTORIA.   Tommy dropped a toy car somewhere, you haven't seen it? It's red. He says it's his best one. Oh the hell with it. Martin's reading him a story. There, isn't it quiet?

            They sit on the bench, holding hands.

EDWARD.   I like women.

VICTORIA.   That should please mother.

EDWARD.   No listen Vicky. I'd rather be a woman. I wish
I had breasts like that, I think they're
beautiful. Can I touch them?

VICTORIA.   What, pretending they're yours?

EDWARD.   No, I know it's you.

VICTORIA.   I think I should warn you I'm enjoying this.

EDWARD.   I'm sick of men.

VICTORIA.   I'm sick of men.

EDWARD.   I think I'm a lesbian.

Scene Three

The park. Summer night. VICTORIA, LIN *and* EDWARD
drunk.

LIN.   Where are you?

VICTORIA.   Come on.

EDWARD.   Do we sit in a circle?

VICTORIA.   Sit in a triangle.

EDWARD.   You're good at mathematics. She's good at
mathematics.

VICTORIA.   Give me your hand. We all hold hands.

EDWARD.   Do you know what to do?

LIN.   She's making it up.

VICTORIA.   We start off by being quiet.

EDWARD.   What?

LIN.   Hush.

EDWARD.   Will something appear?

VICTORIA.   It was your idea.

EDWARD.   It wasn't my idea. It was your book.

women, I don't understand Edward but never
mind.

GERRY.   I'm very involved with him.

BETTY.   I think Edward did try to tell me once but I
didn't listen. So what I'm being told now is that
Edward is 'gay' is that right? And you are too.
And I've been making rather a fool of myself.
But Edward does also sleep with women.

GERRY.   He does, yes, I don't.

BETTY.   Well people always say it's the mother's fault
but I don't intend to start blaming myself. He
seems perfectly happy.

GERRY.   I could still come and see you.

BETTY.   So you could, yes. I'd like that. I've never tried
to pick up a man before.

GERRY.   Not everyone's gay.

BETTY.   No, that's lucky isn't it.

GERRY goes. CLIVE comes.

CLIVE.   You are not that sort of woman, Betty. I can't
believe you are. I can't feel the same about
you as I did. And Africa is to be communist I
suppose. I used to be proud to be British.
There was a high ideal. I came out onto the
verandah and looked at the stars.

*CLIVE goes. BETTY from Act One comes. BETTY
and BETTY embrace.*